✓ THE BIRDMAN OF LAUDERDALE

Clay Christensen

Levins Publishing is grateful to the *Park Bugle*, St. Paul, MN, for permission to use versions of Clay Christensen's articles for the stories in this book.

"Purple Sandpiper Road Trip" appears by permission from the Waukegan Port District *Habor Echo*, Waukegan, IL.

Cover photograph by Chase Vanderbilt.

Cover and book design by Connie Kuhnz.

Composition by Bookmobile Design and Digital Publisher Services Minneapolis, Minnesota

Levins Publishing
2300 Kennedy Street Northeast
Suite 160
MINNEAPOLIS MN 55413
612-238-0989
www.LevinsPublishing.com

ISBN 978-0-9853972-4-1

LCCN: 2013944443

To my wife Jean,
who first called me the Birdman of Lauderdale

Contents

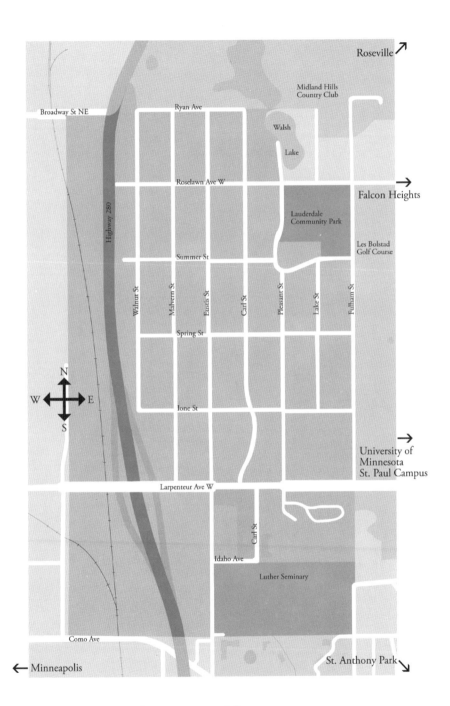

LAUDERDALE, MINNESOTA

✓ The Birdman of Lauderdale

Clay Christensen

"Hello, Sweetie!"

How I Became the Birdman of Lauderdale

Allow me to introduce myself. I'm the self-proclaimed "Birdman of Lauderdale."

Well, not really self-proclaimed. My wife Jean gave me the name several years ago. I live in Lauderdale, a seven by seven block suburb of St. Paul with 2,300 souls near the St. Paul campus of the University of Minnesota. Incorporated in 1949, Lauderdale is an island of modest homes in the Twin Cities metro area. Its borders include two large golf courses with lots of big oaks and other trees, perfect for birds and other wildlife. How I got the Birdman name begins with a St. Paul Audubon bird count.

Since 1900, sometime between Christmas and New Year's Day each year, volunteers throughout the western hemisphere survey pre-assigned fifteen-mile diameter circles, counting all the birds they can find in a twenty-four hour period.

In Minnesota at that time of the year, especially in the Twin Cities, as Minneapolis and St. Paul are known, counters find lots of rock pigeons (the fancy birdwatcher name for pigeons), crows, and house sparrows. But there are always surprises—like a great blue heron that's stayed beyond its usual migration date or a prairie falcon swooping past some grain elevators trying to pick off a rock pigeon for lunch. Volunteers list the species they see. Then they count, or in some cases, estimate the number of individuals in each species. That gets dicey when a flock of starlings goes winging past. "What do you think? Twenty-seven? Thirty-two?" someone will say.

In the evening, we always gather at someone's home for a potluck supper to compare notes, swap tales, and tell lies about what we saw or thought we saw. You can tell it was a slow bird count when people start to claim, "We spotted three pink flamingoes!" Local chapter results are tabulated and sent to state and national coordinators for an annual report.

It's not a scientific count, but I believe it serves a purpose. There's more than anecdotal evidence that this volunteer count sounded the early warning that something was affecting the population of peregrine falcons some forty years ago. Field studies discovered that DDT in the food chain caused thin eggshells and led to severe mortality among peregrines, eagles, and other birds of prey whose diet concentrated this pesticide in their tissues.

In preparation for one particular Christmas count, I spent most of a December Saturday calling folks, lining up volunteers, pairing beginners with more experienced birders, assigning territories, and the like. The phone rang, and Jean answered it. "Somebody wants to speak with the 'Birdman of Lauderdale!'" she called down the hall.

I was sure it was one of the volunteers returning my call, so I answered with the phrase we birders use to mimic the call of the barred owl: "Who cooks for you?"

The deep male voice on the other end answered, "Nobody! She divorced me two years ago!"

It was our friend Harry calling to ask about placing a bird feeder on his deck. He wanted to know what kind of feeder, what type of seed to buy, and what kinds of birds to expect. Luckily, Harry understands my sense of humor.

Since then, I've been the Birdman of Lauderdale.

Hooked on Birds

"Yeah, so what?" I thought to myself when the leader of one of my first birdwatching field trips pointed out a sparrow. "Sparrows are a dime a dozen."

I soon learned otherwise. The man wasn't looking at a common English house sparrow. His sighting was a field sparrow, one of the more than fifteen species of native sparrows commonly found in Minnesota. We'd heard its soft sweet whistles, and then he'd found one. That day I also was surprised to learn that more than three hundred different species of birds can be seen in Minnesota at some point during a given year.

Early on, I discovered the best way to learn about birds wasn't just to get out there and look for them, but to do it with someone who knew what they were looking at. That meant signing up for bird-watching field trips. But a lunchtime stroll with Jean got me into birdwatching in the first place.

At the time, I worked as a computer programmer, not far from Lake Como, an inner city lake in St. Paul. Once in a while, on a spring or summer's day, Jean would join me for a noontime walk around the lake. It's very popular with joggers, dog walkers and love-struck couples . . . we didn't have a dog at the time and weren't joggers . . . and we'd been married nearly twenty-five years.

Several days in a row, we noticed some large black birds coming in over the trees and landing on the lake. Were they loons, Minnesota's state bird? That would be pretty spectacular. We needed to take a closer look. The next day, I brought along my binoculars and a field guide and watched the birds as they approached. There were three or four of them. I decided they looked like double-crested cormorants. In the middle of the city. How common was that?

I found the number for the St. Paul Audubon Society and gave them a call. I got a reply in a couple hours and discussed with a volunteer what I thought I'd seen. She allowed that having cormorants in the middle of the city would be unusual, but it wasn't unheard of. Well, I thought it was pretty special.

After that, Jean and I decided we needed to find out more about birds, see about going on a field trip, go to a meeting, and maybe even think about joining Audubon. All this precipitated our very first field trip in search of owls at Elm Creek Park Reserve, west of the Twin Cities metro. This St. Paul Audubon Society trip began just at sunset. As we drove into the park, we passed a grassy area with a couple of birdhouses on posts and spotted an eastern bluebird. I'd never seen a bluebird. I didn't even know they showed up in Minnesota. My first bird on this first Audubon field trip was a life bird. Wow! This was really great.

Everyone gathered on the Information Center's deck, watching birds come and go at the many bird feeders around the building. Suddenly, someone shouted and pointed toward the tree line: "Pileated woodpecker!" Another life bird! This crow-sized, black and white woodpecker was in undulating flight across the meadow. As we all stood wondering what could top that, we heard an owl call in the distance. "That was a barred owl," someone said. "Its call sounds like 'Who cooks for you?'" Holy cats! A barred owl, the target of our field trip. I would really like to see a barred owl, I thought.

By the time the sun set, a dozen of us were assembled on the deck. The leader hoped we'd hear or maybe see both a barred and a great horned owl. He told us he would use taped owl calls as well as his own vocalizations to try to get a response from one or more of the owls. We had to be quiet on the trail and use our flashlights to avoid stumbling.

Our little group of twelve headed out in a loose single file. Every so often, the leader would bring us to a stop and play his barred owl or great horned owl call. Then we'd all be stone silent in hopes of a response . . . nothing. He repeated the call three or four times at each stop with no luck. After several tries with the tape, he tried his own vocalization of the call. He cupped his hands around his mouth and let out a "Who cooks for you? Who cooks for you-all?" It sounded pretty darned good to me, but again there was no response, except for a dog barking in the distance.

When a few of his own hoots proved fruitless, he showed us one more technique. He explained that owls are sometimes attracted to the squealing of a mouse in distress, thinking they might be able to snatch it from a smaller predator for an easy snack. He raised his hand to pursed lips and made high-pitched kissing sounds against the back of his hand.

We all watched the sky and listened intently in the dark, but still didn't see or hear anything. We hiked a long looping trail and wound up back at the Information Center totally skunked. I was pretty disappointed. On the long drive home, I told Jean that with some practice, I thought I could do that vocalization.

For the next several weeks on my way to and from work, I rolled up the car windows and practiced, "Who cooks for you?" Any passing driver must have wondered what I was hooting about.

A month or so later, Jean and I drove back out to the park. We took the trail that led down to the creek and found a downed log, a likely place to sit. After listening for a little while, I took a deep breath and gave out a fairly timid, "Who cooks for you?" Silence. We waited a minute or two. I tried it again. "Who cooks for you?" Nothing. I was crestfallen. It must have shown on my face.

"Try it again, honey," Jean said.

Another deep breath. "Who cooks for you?"

A response! A real "Who cooks for you?" from a barred owl. It sounded nearby, but we couldn't see it. I made the call again; it replied. We looked up through the trees in the direction of the response, and there was a beautiful barred owl, the first I had ever seen, and certainly the most wonderful one ever created. It was bobbing its head, trying to get a fix on where this call had come from. I called again; it answered again. On my third call, it turned its back, let loose a tremendous volume of whitewash from its perch, and flew off. I wish I knew what I'd said that so insulted it.

Our experience with our first field trip was pretty spectacular and has led to a lifelong passion for me, especially. I can't guarantee your first field trip will ignite the same fire, but I strongly encourage you to give a guided field trip a chance to work its magic for you.

Birds of Retirement

A friend gave me a wire-bound blank book for my retirement. The next day this new journal stared up at me from the kitchen table. Over breakfast, I had an idea: How about logging all the birds I saw each day from the kitchen window? I christened the journal "The Birds of Retirement." I soon became, and continue to be, religious (read "obsessive-compulsive") about recording my bird visitors in it each day.

This journaling of birds is different from the bird lists that other birdwatchers and I might keep. Most of us have some kind of a checklist with a tick mark for each bird we've seen, keeping a cumulative tally. We also usually have at least a life list of the first sighting of each species, or what we call life birds, aka "lifers." I keep both a world life list (1,039 so far) and a Minnesota life list (314).

But there are many other kinds of lists. Some people keep a list for each county. Some start a new list on the first of January each year to track each first sighting of a species. Then there's the yard list, listing everything you've seen in or from your yard. You're able to tell at a glance whether you've ever seen a brown creeper in your yard before, and you can track over time how many different birds you've seen.

My birding friend Ron claims to maintain a "dream" list of the birds he dreams about. I think he also has an albino bird list for every albinistic bird he's seen. Ron has an active imagination and a droll sense of humor. Renowned Minnesota birdwatcher Bob Janssen once said that he keeps sixteen lists, including one he began in 1949 to record the birds he sees each January first.

With my "retirement" journal, I start a new entry every day. This method doesn't work like a list. It's not as easy to determine what birds I have or haven't seen yet when I thumb through my journal. And there's no simple count tally, but a year's worth of journal entries can tell me things that a checklist can't.

For example, every year in early May, I look forward to recording the birds I see during the spring migration. We've had some pretty dramatic waves of warbler migrants come through in past years. They all make it into this journal. Many folks also keep a journal of what they see in their yard day to day. A calendar with ample space by each date can serve as an effective yard journal. It's a good way to get youngsters interested in observing nature. I like looking back in my journal to see when the first hummingbird arrived the year before, so I can plan for its arrival with the nectar feeder filled and ready.

You needn't be as compulsive as some of us. It's just fun to keep a record for a while, maybe a year, to see what's happening in your neighborhood. If you maintain a yard journal from year to year, you may begin to recognize changes in early arrivals or delayed departures or species you're not seeing as frequently or at all. That might lead you to suspect climate effects or habitat changes somewhere in the species' life cycle, maybe right there in your own backyard.

Back when I began birdwatching, I used a pocket-sized spiral notebook to keep track of the birds I saw. I'd list everything: robins, house sparrows, crows—just a listing fool. Then I began to discriminate a bit and listed only species I hadn't seen before.

After I had a hundred or so birds in my notebook, I found a hardcovered "Life List and Diary." This book is now my "official" record of all the bird species I've seen in North America. It has preprinted space for entering date, locality, habitat, and notes on four species on each of its two hundred pages. Reading through it, I can conjure up where I was and with whom when I first saw a given bird.

As for a pocket-sized spiral notebook, I've stopped using one when I'm on a tropical bird trip. It really hit home on one trip just why making entries in a notebook on the trail was more frustration than I needed. When birding in the tropics, every bird I see is a new bird. The guide points to a bird, calls out the name, and while I write that in my notebook, he points to two or three more and calls out their names. Then I'm left asking, "What was that? What did he say?" And the birds often come fast and furious, with ten or more new birds while you're standing in one spot. Sometimes they're just a silhouette against the skyline.

Before a trip like this, I don't take the time to study all the birds we might see. I should, but I don't. In one case, the field guide I bought for our September 2006 Ecuador trip had six pages of hummingbirds with thirty birds per page! Trying to study them and memorize distinguishing field marks would have overwhelmed me.

About halfway through the Ecuador trip, I began to feel stupid just writing down bird names. Was I really birdwatching? Or was I merely a stenographer, writing down what another person had spotted and identified? Was this what birdwatching should be about? How could I boast about spotting two hundred and sixteen new birds in Ecuador, when I couldn't have identified more than a handful without help?

Sinking into a mild depression, I pulled aside my birding buddy Bill and told him I didn't think I'd ever make a trip like this again. Bill didn't really reply. Instead, he just kind of mumbled, and we went on to the next bird. Later, I wished that he or someone had challenged me because I really hadn't thought through my reasons for not wanting to do a trip like that again.

In December of the same year, I got word that another trip to Ecuador was being planned, with most of the same fun gang of scoundrels from the previous trip. This time, however, I wasn't sure I wanted to go. I decided to call Craig Thompson, Regional Land Program Supervisor for the Wisconsin Department of Natural Resources, the fellow who's put these trips together for over a decade, and had a heart-to-heart with him. I told him I felt like a phony, that I couldn't identify most of those birds even if they were to perch on the open page of my guidebook. I felt like a scribe just writing down what people told me. Craig understood how I felt and asked, "What would it take to change that feeling?"

"Well," I replied, "if I didn't have to keep that damn list. What's the point?"

Craig told me what I secretly wanted to hear: He suggested not keeping a list. He'd found that it detracted from the time spent actually watching a bird, valuable time he could use to admire a bird's features and habits. He himself had quit listing the birds he sees in the tropics and just enjoys them and the ambiance of the habitat. "Absorbing the gestalt experience," as he calls it. At the end of each day, his birding group always compiles a checklist. That's all he uses when he wants to look back to determine what he's seen and where.

Not keep a list? That smacked of heresy. How could I consider such a thing? But I had to admit that his suggestion and the possibility of a major birding trip without keeping a bird-by-bird list sounded wonderfully liberating.

And so, that was my resolution: to go to Ecuador that next summer and try out a new approach to birdwatching. No list, no guilt. Just enjoy the trip, the group, the scenery and, of course, the birds.

Little Adventures

Gregarious as I am, I really enjoy birding by myself, too. It's a great time for solitude, reflection, and communing with nature. I find a likely spot, in the shade, if possible, and just sit there and see what comes by.

I like the serendipity of leaving the birdwatching to chance. I'm not on a quest for a reported rare bird. I'm just content to see what there is to be seen, appreciating even the more common birds and really feeling blessed when some rare or unusual bird comes into view. One disadvantage, however, is that I don't get to share any of my rarer sightings with someone immediately or, what's important for me, receive any on-site help with identification of a questionable sighting.

Before I retired, I occasionally had the wonderful experience of gazing out my office window overlooking Long Meadow Lake in Bloomington, south of Minneapolis, and seeing a flock of pelicans perform an aerial ballet. They moved in unison, high in the air, like a mobile, and when they turned "on edge" they seemed to disappear for a moment. I'd call out to my officemates, "Hey, pelicans! Over there!" and already the birds would've turned so that none of the people I summoned could see them for a moment or two.

In my early and most enthusiastic birding days, I spent many an early weekend morning down the block and around the corner on the shores of Walsh Lake, a lovely little Lauderdale lake. I'd sit there for an hour or so, watching eastern kingbirds, kingfishers, wood ducks, and an occasional shorebird during migration. One winter morning I even got to see a red-bellied woodpecker looking down at me from high above on a branch. When a breeze fluffed its feathers, it allowed about the only view where I could see the red undercover of down on its belly that gives him his name.

Jean and I didn't always see many birds when we hiked through the dense woods in Afton State Park on the pristine St. Croix River, but one time we had quite a surprise. As we came around a bend on the edge of a field, some deer hiding in the grasses heard us. A couple of loud snorts really made us jump. It was awesome to watch a big buck and two does hightail it across the prairie.

Soon after Jean's and my inaugural St. Paul Audubon field trip to Elm Creek Park Reserve, we returned one evening to see if we could attract a barred owl. In the moments of sitting and waiting for an owl to respond to my calls, Jean noticed something furry sticking out of a hole up in a tree. We soon realized it was a raccoon's tail. As we continued to watch, a young raccoon got himself turned around and crawled out. Two siblings soon followed him. Besides eventually seeing the barred owl, we got to observe three young raccoons just waking up for their nocturnal prowl.

South of the Cities, Murphy Hanrahan Park used to be one of my favorite haunts. This huge park covers many acres and extends into both Scott and Dakota Counties. One Sunday morning, just as I stepped out of a port-a-potty, I noticed a phoebe, a kind of fly-catcher, perched on a small tree on the edge of the woods, not ten feet from me. I stood stock-still. Then I raised my outstretched right arm oh-so-slowly toward the phoebe. The bird fluttered toward me and landed on my forearm. It took flight to grab a fly and then landed back on my upper arm. It was one of the most exceptional experiences I've ever had. (And I resent any suggestion that the bird thought he was going to find a lot of flies around me!)

Sunrise Pool is part of the Carlos Avery Wildlife Management Area north of St. Paul. I used to go out there on a Saturday morning and just sit to see what would fly by. One October morning I had what I consider a private fall warbler tutorial. Many of the beautiful, colorful, warblers we see in the spring become drab and silent in the fall.

One of the challenges in birdwatching is learning to identify what several bird guides call "Confusing Fall Warblers." That morning I watched wave after wave of warblers come through as I quietly sat on a fallen trunk. Although I seldom got to see an entire bird at a time, I did get enough good looks at a head here, a tail there, or a wing bar to be able to piece together firm identifications. It was like having a private tutorial on confusing fall warblers by the best teachers in the world.

Sunrise Pool is the same place my buddy Bill and I once saw an ermine cross the road. It was dressed in its winter costume, all in white with a black tip on its tail, and didn't seem to notice us at all. One December day, he and I also discovered a rare and elusive Townsend's solitaire along an icy stream in the Sunrise Pool section. This bird usually shows up somewhere in Minnesota every year, but to stumble upon one in winter, and then to successfully identify it (a remarkably plain looking bird) was a high-five moment for us.

Another place I always enjoyed early on a weekend morning was Fort Snelling State Park along the Mississippi in St. Paul. One morning, I sat on the edge of a hiking path waiting for a bird to show up when a ground hog lumbered by. It sniffed at a few things, found a plant it seemed to like, sat, and munched on that for a while, paying no attention to me. Another day as I walked along a path, I noticed a young skunk following me on the other side. I stood very still, got my camera ready, and snapped a half dozen shots as it ambled by. I don't think it even knew I was there. It had something else on its mind.

One problem I learned to address fairly quickly while birdwatching was where to go to the bathroom. Again, at Fort Snelling State Park on a Sunday morning, I was on a path along the Minnesota River when the urge came over me. I headed down into the trees lining the river toward a clear area along the riverbank. I turned to face the path, putting a tree between myself and anyone who might happen along on the trail. As I was mid-stream, so to speak, I heard a rush of water behind me, like the river had suddenly developed a tide. I looked over my shoulder and froze. There was a riverboat with dozens of people on both decks, with a banner proclaiming

"St. Paul Days on the River." I tried to remain motionless, a posture that serves me well in nature, and nobody laughed or pointed, so I may have gone undetected. But I knew better than to choose such an exposed spot in the future.

A similar subject came up as part of a birding class I helped facilitate. My friend Carol held a beginners' birding class that consisted of a Saturday field trip sandwiched between two nights of classroom lecture. We got through the first class, had the field trip, and then gathered for the second night's class the following week. After reviewing what we'd seen and covering a few other topics, Carol asked if there were any questions about the field trip.

"Well, yes," one woman asked timidly. "How do you go to the bathroom out there? We were out four hours. That's an awfully long time to have to hold it."

Carol replied, "Well, you just step off into the woods a ways and then catch up with the group when you're done. Last Saturday, I lagged behind the group for a bit, then headed into the woods, and did anybody see me?"

Three of us guys looked around and slowly raised our hands. Carol turned red from the neck up. We hadn't really seen her, but it was such a perfect setup. A word of caution: If you're going to sneak into the woods on a birdwatching hike, just remember that everyone else has binoculars.

My back deck is one of my favorite places to wait and see what flies by. It's only about ten by twelve feet, but there's a very clear patch of sky above it. One fall morning I was sitting out there with my neighbor Jim, chatting and sipping coffee, when I saw a swirl of pepper dots high above us in the northern sky. I ran in, got my binocs, and confirmed that it was a kettle of broad-winged hawks migrating south. Broad-wings swirl upwards on thermals, saving a great deal of energy, and as the thermal begins to fade, they peel off in single file to find the next updraft and continue their southerly journey.

Another day on the deck I spotted a flock of Canada geese come into view. I usually don't bother to give a flock of Canada geese more than a passing glance, but for some reason I decided to look at this one a little more closely. I often compulsively count the birds in a flock just to keep in practice for the Christmas Bird Count. This "V" of Canada geese had a surprise in store for this jaded birdwatcher. At the end of one of the legs of the V was a white pelican. I'd sure like to have heard his story. "Just hangin' out with my goose buddies. . . ."

Incidentally, that reminds me of one of birdwatching's most perplexing questions: "Do you know why, when you see a flock of geese fly over, one leg of the V is longer than the other?"

In case you haven't heard this one before, it's because there are more geese in the longer leg.

Joshua Goes Birding

Normally, I wouldn't volunteer to take a twelve-year old shopping. But one time I did. I got a lot more than I expected.

Over the course of a couple of months, my grandson Joshua and I planned a birding trip to the Villa Maria Retreat and Conference Center, downriver from the Twin Cities near the small town of Frontenac overlooking the Mississippi River. Every Mother's Day weekend, the St. Paul Audubon Society rents the entire Center for its annual Warbler Weekend.

One Saturday before the big event, Josh and I went out to get him some gear for the trip. First, we stopped at a bookstore for a birding field guide. After some browsing, we settled on a Peterson's guide for the east and central United States. I like Peterson's because it uses paintings rather than photographs. The artist emphasizes what's unique about a bird as a species; a photograph of one individual might not include some traits of the species as a whole. Peterson also uses arrows to highlight diagnostic features, so you have a quick reference to aid in bird identification. Having the descriptive text near the illustration is very handy in the field.

After buying the field guide, we continued outfitting Josh at Fleet Farm. We bought a pair of Wellingtons, knee-high boots perfect for the mud we'd probably have down on Sand Point where Wells Creek flows across its muddy delta into the Mississippi. We also found a green rain suit, jacket and pants, just in case. After Josh picked out a brown, floppy, broad-brimmed hat from the American

Museum of National History, he was prepared for rain or shine. I looked for a compass and a whistle, something he could use in the remote prospect that we got separated on the trail. A combination whistle, compass, magnifying glass, and thermometer on a key chain arrangement did the trick. He was thrilled. Now, if he got lost, he'd know how cold he was, too!

Next we hit the stationery section and found a small waterproof spiral notebook to record his sightings and a package of three erasable ballpoint pens. They had to be erasable because, "They're so cool, Grandpa!"

All set, we checked out and headed home. At the corner of two cross streets near where I live, mallards and Canada geese often swim in little Healy Pond. As we rounded the corner, I said, "Now, look in the pond, Josh. There could be some birds."

"Grandpa, I see a swan or something! A big white bird!"

I pulled into the church lot next to the pond. "It's an egret," he exclaimed. "Where's my notebook?"

We had to get this first sighting documented. I reached back and swung the Fleet Farm bag up from the back seat. He dove into the bag and brought out the spiral notebook and the set of erasable pens. Prying a pen from the package, he began to write.

"Now, put down the date," I coached, "and the location, Healy Pond, Roseville." He made the first entry in his birding life list, "Great egret," followed immediately by "Wood ducks, ♂ and ♀." He assured me that he knew the symbols for male and female, bringing a smile to my face and my heart.

When we got back home, we sat on the front steps and watched the bird feeders. He proudly added chickadee, white-breasted nuthatch, and house finch to his life list.

I hoped I'd sparked a lifetime interest in this young lad. I'd consider that a significant accomplishment, a kind of "life list" that matters most.

Hello, Sweetie

After nearly fifty years of marriage, my wife and I have devised a number of ways to communicate with each other. One is to softly whistle a four-note phrase that sounds like "Hello, Sweetie." "Hello" is two low notes, which then rise on the "swee" and go back down on the "tee."

Jean doesn't usually carry her cell phone, so we use this four-note whistle when we're roaming through different aisles of a big box store looking for each other. When I hear that tune, I stop to figure out where it's coming from and head in that direction.

One morning I was out with our dog Buffy in the back alley when I heard Jean's soft whistle. What the heck was going on? If Jean wanted to tell me the phone was for me, why didn't she use the garden bell outside the back door and clang it a few times? (Like Pavlov's dog, I also respond to bells.) With my interest piqued, I hurried toward the house where I saw Jean leaning out the bedroom window, frantically waving.

"What's up?" I asked.

"That big bird is back!" she stage-whispered. "The one we saw yesterday. Out front. It's here again!"

I went in the side door so Buffy wouldn't bound around the corner of the house. I didn't want him rushing into the front yard, where he might spook the bird. While hustling to get to the front window, I considered the large bird we'd seen the day before. It had grabbed a smaller bird out of a shrub right next to the front window and had carried it to a tree. We'd decided it was a sharp-shinned hawk, based on a fleeting glance at its size. I also thought I saw the black and white pattern of a hapless junco in its clutches. Was today's bird the same hungry one from yesterday, or was this a new visitor?

When I arrived at the front window, Jean quickly updated me. The bird she'd seen in the same shrub was now perched in our neighbor's mountain ash tree. It looked more like a Cooper's hawk, larger than the sharp-shinned, but with a similar appetite for eating other birds.

These two accipiters, as they're called, are probably the toughest raptors for me to identify. Each of my hawk identification guidebooks has a bookmark stuck in the sharpie and Cooper's sections. I pull them off the shelf every time I see either of them and compare my visual notes to the photos and descriptions in the books.

I was pretty convinced that the hawk Jean had spotted was a Cooper's hawk: The large size, rounded tail, and strong white terminal band at the end of the tail were my clues. We managed to get a good look at it. Since it had thrashed the same bush as yesterday's hawk, I believed we were seeing the same one. After its success the day before, it had come back for another chance.

Just then a deliveryman at the neighbor's house spooked it. It flew about thirty feet to the Juneberry tree outside our kitchen window. After a pause, it dropped to the sidewalk at the corner of the house. I had no idea what it was going after, but one time we had a Cooper's snatch a vole out of the yard. And with birdseed scattered under the feeders in the front of the house, an unlucky rodent may have been in the hawk's sights.

Witnessing an accipiter grab a bird out of the yard reminds me that bird feeders are bird feeders, whether the food is seed or bird—a grim reality in nature. As Jean says, "It seems everything is food for something else."

Song of Myself

One spring an entire issue of the Virginia Quarterly Review was devoted to Walt Whitman. One article explored the relationship between the brags of the early West—the boastings of the river men and barge deck hands—and Whitman's poetry. In that light, Whitman's poem "Song of Myself" was less a conceited, self-centered rant and more like a "brag" about himself and his country.

While I don't pretend to understand much poetry, the idea resonated with me as a birder. It occurred to me that when a bird sings, he's really singing the song of himself. I say "he" because it's almost always the male who sings.

Birds' vocalizations are usually divided into songs and calls. Songs are for declaring territory, for attracting a mate, and just for the pleasure of expression. Songs are linked to the hormonal cycles that birds go through. They're also related to light levels: Listen for the dawn and dusk choruses. My wife and I contend that robins never want to go to bed. They're always the last ones singing as light fades from our neighborhood.

One of the main reasons a bird sings is to declare territorial boundaries. I once watched a meadowlark fly from fencepost to fencepost, singing his heart out at each stop. He was singing, "This is my territory." Off to the next post. "And this is, too!" In a sense, song is a bird's method of confrontation. Yes, birds do sometimes physically drive other birds out of their territory. But in the main, they declare their boundaries with song. Isn't that cool? I imagine it's the kind of a battle poets would fight, slinging poetry at each other.

When a male bird sings to attract a mate, he usually chooses a prominent perch from which to demonstrate his vocal prowess. The female listens to see if the song is sung correctly, with suitable vigor and volume. Larks and bobolinks, which nest in open fields, don't have many good singing perches, so they sing their songs while hovering in the air. Some female birds sing, too, but usually not a full territorial song. Some thrushes, dippers, wrens, orioles, tanagers and finches, the northern cardinal, and rose-breasted grosbeak females sing songs every bit as complex as their male counterparts.

What I love is antiphonal singing, songs that alternate between a mated pair of birds. The male and female sing them one at a time—sometimes different songs, sometimes the same. It's thought that antiphonal singing is useful in reinforcing pair bonds, especially in dense habitats. Birds that sing antiphonally include the bobwhite and brown-headed cowbird. Bobwhites are found east of the Rockies and as far north as extreme southeastern Minnesota. Cowbirds cover the entire United States.

Birds use what is called a "whisper song" or "subsong" in the presence of a threat to let others know there's danger without attracting attention. Some also use soft songs around the nest to avoid revealing its location. Parents sing around their nest as the youngsters prepare to fledge. The theory is that birds are born with the basic, generic song pattern for their species. But listening to the singing of the adults helps them learn the details and variations of their songs, how to sing them "correctly."

I get a kick out of hearing juvenile white-throated sparrows practice their songs during their first fall migration. They'll get two out of three phrases right, but really miss it on the third. The mnemonic memory phrase we birdwatchers use for the white-throated sparrow song is "Poor Sam Peabody, Peabody, Peabody." But the youngsters sound like "Poor Sam Pubbidy, Pubbidy." And they lose volume as they lose confidence. Even the next spring, the newbies are still trying to get it right. Listen for the rookies in both fall and spring.

Some birds demonstrate variety, especially those classified as mimics. The brown thrasher, catbird, some thrushes, and the northern mockingbird are mimics that borrow songs and sounds from a variety of sources. Their prospective mates are probably looking for variety of repertoire.

We have a blue jay in the neighborhood that faked me out with his excellent red-tailed hawk imitation. I heard the high-pitched descending call, heard in every Western movie as the hero steps out of the saloon. I looked up for the hawk and saw only the blue jay in the tree above me. As I watched, he repeated his mimicry. I suspect he does it to scare off his competition for food—and just for the fun of it.

Sometimes singing is an expression of plain exuberance. That's an easy conclusion when you watch a cardinal throw back his head and sing his heart out. It appears to be an emotional release. It's also likely that the mimics who imitate others' songs and concoct their own "concertos" are not only demonstrating their facility, but having fun as well.

Calls are different from songs. Calls are signals used for warning, defense, and distress, uttered as needed. They're usually not musical. The call of the boreal owl determines if it's safe to return to the nest. The male will call from a distance. If the nest area is safe to approach, the female will respond to him. If she doesn't answer, he doesn't come in. He'll repeat the call until he gets the okay to return. Nestlings use calls to beg for food. Birds use very brief short calls or chips to keep in touch with each other, providing flock cohesion during migration. Calls are also used while foraging to identify a food source. A mother bird with a brood of chicks uses a gathering call to keep them together and a warning call to bring them to safety.

Calls are signals, songs are for territory, finding a mate, and—my favorite—just for the fun of it. When I hear a bird in song, like the brags of Walt Whitman, I feel he's singing the song of himself.

My Spanish Lesson

One time I had the pleasure and privilege of spending ten very full days birdwatching in Ecuador. In preparation I took ten weeks of Spanish lessons, hoping to be able to communicate with the locals.

At the least, I joked, I wanted to be able to say, "Please don't kidnap me! I'm not rich! Take him!" while pointing at Bill, who was also going on the trip. Luckily, we had no such encounters.

Located on the northwestern "shoulder" of South America, Ecuador sits astride the equator. It's about the size of Colorado, with a population of about 13.5 million. The Andes Mountains form the central north-south spine of the country, flanked by the Amazon jungle on the east and Pacific coastal lowlands on the west. Most flights from the United States to Ecuador land in Quito, the capital, in the northern part of the country, right on the equator.

Our flight landed around midnight. Then we were up early for breakfast in the hotel and another flight to a couple of reserves in southern Ecuador. We flew south along the eastern edge of the Andes, looking at snow-capped mountains. Some, though not all, were dormant volcanoes. We searched for a glimpse of the largest bird in the Americas, the Andean condor. No such luck. Landing in Catamayo, the airport for the city of Loja, was fairly exciting. The airport sits at the bottom of a "bowl" of Andean peaks. Landing requires a steep banking and diving maneuver, not for the faint of heart. I was stunned to learn later that only the top ten pilots in Ecuador, ours thankfully among them, are allowed to land in Catamayo because of its geography.

Our trip wasn't only for birdwatching. It also served as a fundraiser for the Jocotoco Foundation, an organization that manages seven wild-life reserves in Ecuador. As a part of the cost of the trip, each birder contributed an additional $500. We also took pledges from friends and family for the foundation to use toward the purchase of more land to protect habitat.

We spent three or four days each at two of the Jocotoco reserves in southern Ecuador. The first was on Mount Tapichalaca, which rises 8,000 feet on the eastern side of the Andes. This wet and rainy region is good for maintaining a rain forest ecosystem, but not so good for hikers who want to stay dry and catch a glimpse of some rare birds. On one of the high hiking trails, however, we were lucky to find the endangered Jocotoco antpitta, the bird for which the foundation was created and named. The bird's soft call sounds like a repeated "Hoko, toko."

Robert S. Ridgely, the artist for the voluminous *Birds of Ecuador* guidebook, discovered and named the bird in 1997. The Jocotoco antpitta is extremely shy and is thought to exist only in the southern Ecuador reserve where it was first found. This bird is nine inches tall, pudgy with a very short tail. It walks upright and looks like a small football on sticks.

The second half of our trip, we stayed at Buenaventura Lodge on the Andes' western slope at just 3,000 feet. The climate in this area has less rain than the east side, but there's just as much fog and mist. The lodges in both locations had full bathrooms attached to each of the bedrooms. At my advanced age, that's really important.

Back home in one of my first Spanish lessons, I'd learned that "¡Mucho gusto!" meant, "Pleased to meet you!" Somehow I came to believe that "gusto" meant to "like" something. So naturally, I reasoned that "mucho gusto" should mean "I like it a lot."

During the first several days of our stay at the Tapichalaca Lodge, I used "¡mucho gusto!" at every meal to express how much I enjoyed the food. As we passed by the kitchen staff to reach the stairway to our bedrooms, I told them all, "¡Mucho gusto!" to let them know how great the meal was.

After four days of this, I found myself sitting next to Betty at lunch. She'd spent three years in Ecuador while in the Peace Corps. She leaned over and said matter-of-factly, "You know, when you say, '¡Mucho gusto!' you're really saying, 'Pleased to meet you!'"

"But I meant to say 'I liked it a lot!'"

"Then you should probably say, '¡Me gusta!'" she explained.

"You mean, when I finished that dessert and wanted to tell the server how great it was, I was saying, 'Oh, that dessert. Pleased to meet you'?"

"Yes," she said, "that's what you've been saying." I was so embarrassed!

Sadly chastened, I switched to "¡Me gusta!," and the looks I got from the staff seemed much more comfortable. Until, that is, the last day at Buenaventura Lodge on the western side of the mountains.

The kitchen helpers, who also waited the tables, were the same men who loaded our luggage onto the bus. I wanted to let them know, now that we were leaving, how much I'd enjoyed my stay at the lodge, the food, the birds, and the scenery. I figured I could add a "mucho" to the phrase and really emphasize how much I liked being there. So, I said to each of them, "¡Me gusta mucho!" when I passed them as they loaded the luggage at the back of the bus.

As I was about to climb the steps into the bus, our guide José gently pulled me aside and asked, "Do you know what you said to those guys?"

"I thought I said that I had liked it here very much," I replied.

"No. You said, 'I like YOU very much!'" he told me, making no attempt to stifle his laughter.

With José beside me, I retraced my steps to the rear of the bus. There stood the three guys with puzzled looks on their faces. I dramatically blew them a kiss. That cracked them up, and we all convulsed in laughter.

So much for my Spanish lessons. I thought I deserved a refund or at least remedial lessons.

Job Corps Birders

I really get a kick out of introducing people, especially kids, to birdwatching. One time I got a kick raised to the eighth power.

It started with a request from my neighbor Renee who was an instructor at the Humphrey Job Corps Center, a former Bible college, near the State Fair grounds. Would I be willing to come over and share some information about birdwatching? Maybe take a group on a field trip? Would I?

I joined the group around a lunch table at the Job Corps campus one morning for a get-acquainted session. Renee had nicknamed her small class of eighteen to twenty-year-olds the "River Rats." They wanted to be volunteer aides on the "Big River Journey," a paddleboat ride on the Mississippi River sponsored by the National Park Service to get gradeschoolers more involved in nature. Renee's students hoped to help the younger kids learn about birdwatching. They told me they received *The Park Bugle* in their classroom and read my *Birdman of Lauderdale* column every month. Ego boost!

She'd given the kids an illustration from the *Minnesota Conservation Volunteer* magazine showing some two dozen birds. Their assignment was to identify them all, so we worked on that using one of my field guides. When we finished, we made plans for a field trip the following week to the Bass Ponds in Bloomington, a suburb south of Minneapolis. After I left, Renee asked the group where they'd like to go on their next outing. "Lauderdale!" was the response.

The summer before, Renee started a program called Adventure Club. "I want my students to know that everything is an adventure," she said. "I want them to know that they already know a whole lot, but that knowledge grows exponentially when they apply it to the unknown. It's all about experiential education."

Many of her students had had limited opportunity to experience the joy and peacefulness of nature, but when they were involved in the environment, they got to be the people they wanted to be.

"The pressures of society fall away and they are free," she said. As we exchanged e-mails finalizing our field trip, she noted that her kids usually lasted for just an hour or two. "Their attention has a very short existence," she said. "They're a bit like May flies: very dramatic, but they die off quickly."

I borrowed ten binoculars and field guides from St. Paul Audubon's Youth Mentorship Program and met the group of eight kids early on a drizzly March morning. Renee drove the van, and we headed for the Minnesota Valley National Wildlife Refuge visitor center in Bloomington. The minute we walked in the students headed for the big windows near the bird feeders and were welcomed by a whole passel of turkeys on the other side of the glass. "Wow! They're huge!" someone exclaimed.

Then one young fellow saw a bird flit to the feeder. "There's a white bird!" he shouted. "What's that white bird?"

"Vang," Renee said, addressing the young man, "that's the bird you told me says its name. Remember that one?"

"Oh, yeah," Vang said. "It's a chickadee-dee-dee!"

The students spread out through the visitor center. Some were watching the feeder on the north side of the building when a sharp-shinned hawk swooped in and nailed a downy woodpecker. The hawk worked its prey over on the ground for a few moments and then headed off to a private perch with the bird clutched in its talons. You can't program teachable moments like that.

After we spent a fair amount of time at the visitor center, we decided to forego the hike at the Bass Ponds. It was still drizzling, and we'd have been at the mercy of the elements. So, we headed for one other stop at a bald eagles' nest on the shore of Keller Lake in the St. Paul suburb of Maplewood. The nest looked empty when we got there; I set up my spotting scope to give it a closer look. There, tucked down out of the rain, the back of an eagle's white head poked over the rim of the nest. The students were pretty excited to see even a part of the head of such a magnificent bird. And then, the nest dweller's mate flew in and perched in full view on a nearby branch. Now we could see both the perched bird and the nest in the scope. Again, you can't program sights like that.

Two weeks after our trip, my neighbor sent me a note telling me that she had just taken her eight River Rats out to Mounds Park. She reported that when they were riding along in the van, a student named Randy had said, "I was out with my friends this weekend and, I didn't notice it right away, but I was watching all the birds. I just started birdwatching and I didn't even notice it."

That's the kind of kick I'm talking about.

Taking the Dread out of Winter

As I get older I think more soberly about the approach of the typical Minnesota winter: the cold, the ice, the winds, the short days, and the long nights.

One year my mood was particularly gloomy. Buffy the dog and I had reached the same age. He was going to be seventy in dog years, and I was going to be seventy in human years! Part of my dread was the reminder of the brevity of life in general and of my life in particular. Fortunately, I got welcome relief from my malaise, and it came from an unexpected source—one of our most common birds during what I expected to be a rather mundane field trip.

In late September that year, I was one of several birders who volunteered to take a group of high school students on a bird walk in the wooded area of Como Park, also the home of Como Lake. It was a windy day with a threat of rain, gloomy enough to match my mood. Although our group didn't find a lot of birds, we did get to see some bluebirds chasing each other, a pretty little American redstart (a warbler with oriole-like black and orange markings), several northern flickers, and a flycatcher called an Eastern phoebe.

But the bird that inspired me was a downy woodpecker high up on a dead snag. I could tell it was a male by the red patch on the back of his head, which females lack. Up there on that limbless tree, he was perched just below a perfectly round hole. He sat still for a bit and then darted headfirst into the hole until just the tip of his tail poked out. It turned out he was working on this hole. After a moment or two, he backed himself out.

What was he up to, I wondered? Fall wasn't the right time of the year for nest building. This probably was going to be a roost hole with the entrance facing away from the chilly north wind. Several Minnesota woodpecker species don't migrate, or if they do, they go only short distances. When they find an area with a decent winter food supply and shelter, they generally stay put. Woodpeckers usually sleep alone in a cavity at night and usually make several of them because they compete with chickadees, nuthatches and other woodpeckers, all of which are perfectly happy to squat in a woodpecker roost hole. Imagine, just as winter dusk is falling, you fly up to one of your favorite roost holes, stick your head in and, whammo, an aggressive beak is thrust at your face. Cavity roosting can be a hazardous prospect.

As I watched this little guy, I felt he was teaching me something. Preparing for winter and for what he knew would be cold nights ahead made him too busy to worry about dreading it. That industrious little downy was teaching me not to waste time and energy dreading the inevitable. Even though I could ponder mortality and he couldn't, I wasn't that different from the woodpecker. Pondering mortality didn't give me special coping skills. When confronted with the inevitable, I decided there's only one thing I can do: Prepare for it as best I'm able and then face it squarely. As I thought more about it, my dread lifted. In its place, I made a resolution to prepare, plan, and face winter head-on.

Here are some of my ideas for winter "roosts," places to go for birdwatching and other bird-related activities to ease the pain of the cold season. In the Twin Cities several Audubon chapters and bird clubs offer field trips and other events throughout the winter. Most Audubon chapters in North America sponsor a Christmas Bird Count. They're always looking for participants.

Our Minnesota Ornithologists' Union hosts a "paper" session at the University of Minnesota's Bell Museum each December. Scientists and researchers from all over Minnesota present a summary of their recent work, replete with displays and a fantastic book sale (my downfall). The MOU also has field trips going all winter long.

In general, one of the best places to look for birds is where there's open water. In the Twin Cities, I head to Black Dog Lake at least once during the winter. The heat from the nearby power plant keeps part of the lake open most of the winter, and wintering gulls, ducks, and eagles are often seen. The Twin City portions of the Mississippi River and further south at Lake Pepin are also good places to scout.

As part of my program to avoid the twin dreads of age and winter, I take part in the golden eagle survey in southeastern Minnesota every January. Run by the National Eagle Center in Wabasha (a great place to visit any time), it has resident educational eagles, informative presentations, and great views of eagles on the Mississippi from inside their building and outdoor decks.

Unlike woodpecker roost holes, all of these roosts are big enough to share.

"Backyard Birds"

Chickadee Demise

The black-capped chickadee is one of my favorite birds. It's a perennial feature on seasonal greeting cards, sweatshirts, and in home décor. In Minnesota, most of us see them all year round. It's such a pleasant surprise to be skiing or hiking through a winter woods and hear that "dee-dee-dee-dee" nearby. Look overhead and there's a chickadee come to see who you are, what you're up to, and welcome you to his part of the woods. They're very inquisitive and can be drawn in by imitating their "fee-bee" whistle.

Chickadees can really brighten a winter day with their perky antics as they flit to and fro at a feeder, too. One is often within two or three feet of me when I'm out in the yard. I've even had one land on the platform feeder while I was adding food to the other side. Several friends have had chickadees feed from an outstretched hand.

Watch a chickadee as it eats and you'll notice it takes a seed in its beak, transfers the seed to its feet, and then pecks it open to get at the kernel inside. The chickadee bill isn't built for seed cracking like the beak of a finch or cardinal, so a chickadee holds the seed tight with both feet and pecks away at it. I've always thought it great that chickadees hang around all winter, willing to brave the winter storms, finding a way to survive in our "Arctic" north. But it may not be a matter of choice on the chickadees' part. Given their bulk, they're not able to fly long distances.

One winter morning I was out with Buffy when I noticed a chickadee quietly sitting in the seed tray at the bottom of our tube

feeder. It wasn't pecking at the seeds. It just sat on the sunny side of
the feeder, shivering in the sub-zero air. I had recently read Bernd
Heinrich's *Winter World: The Ingenuity of Animal Survival* and knew
that shivering is one way birds and other creatures keep warm. The
chickadee didn't stir when I walked by. I just figured it was really cold.

When Jean and I sat down for breakfast, I told her about the chickadee resting on the feeder right in front of the window. As I directed
her attention to the tray, we watched the little bird roll onto its back.
Its legs went straight in the air, and its toes curled up.

"That doesn't look good." I said. "I think it's dying."

I rushed outside without a jacket and lifted the bird off the feeder,
hugged it against my body, and hustled back into the house. The bird
seemed unresponsive. I guessed I was too late, but I put it on a towel
on the table in the morning sunlight.

After breakfast, I took the lifeless bird and turned it onto its back.
I puffed lightly at the chest area to lift the feathers to see how much
fat it had stored on its chest area. A chickadee needs to build up its
fat reserves every day because it uses them up almost completely every
winter night just trying to keep warm. I didn't see any whitish-yellow
reserves at all on this little bird. I did feel a lump right at the base
of the chin. I wondered if it were a tumor or an obstruction in its
esophagus that had made it difficult or impossible for it to eat. Maybe
it had died because it had a sunflower seed stuck in there.

I called my friend, Phil Jenni, director of the Wildlife Rehabilitation Center in the nearby suburb of Roseville, and asked if the veterinarian could take a look at it, especially that lump. He said he
was sure the vet would be glad to do so. Phil also told me to keep the
bird in the freezer until I could make it. When I showed it to the vet
the next day, she said the lump I'd felt was merely the bird's throat.
She would examine the bird when it thawed and give me a call.

That afternoon she told me she couldn't find an obvious cause of
death. She agreed that the bird didn't seem to have any fat deposits
and speculated that it just got too cold and couldn't make it. I was
looking for some way to excuse my delay, my not bringing the bird
into the house sooner. But, as Phil told me, wild creatures try not to

show illness: It's a sign of weakness and makes them vulnerable to predators. He added that by the time you can capture a bird or animal, it's probably pretty sick or seriously injured. This chickadee hadn't made any effort to flee when I discovered it.

In chickadee hierarchy the dominant bird gets first crack at the food. So if this little one was low bird on the chickadee totem pole, it may not have been able to get enough food to build the fat reserves it needed to make it through the night. It was frustrating because I had a brand new chickadee roosting box mounted on the garage. Why hadn't this little guy used it during the night? As far as I could tell, no bird made use of it all winter. What's a mother to do?

Through this experience, I learned you can't always tell that a creature's life is in peril. I guess you have to do the best you can with what you know.

Sharpie v. Junco

The adventure began while I was watching Sunday afternoon football from my easy chair. I heard a "whoomp" behind me. Buffy woke up and barked. It sounded like a large bird had glanced off the living room window. The bird quickly recovered and headed off to the north. Could it have been one of the mourning doves I'd seen at the birdbath earlier?

I opened the front door just enough to peek around it. The cocker spaniel squeezed his way out and scouted his ground-level territory. I looked around and saw a sharp-shinned hawk perched on our neighbor Rodd's porch railing. The sharpie is an aggressive hunter with piercing red eyes that stare out from a smallish gunmetal gray head.

As I stood with the storm door slightly ajar, the hawk flew up to Rodd's maple tree and watched Buffy and me. At the same time, I felt something brush past my leg into the house. Oh, oh. Bird, mouse, or what? After I got the pooch back inside, I closed the basement door and all the hallway doors. I told Jean I suspected a bird had gotten in, but I hadn't seen anything.

"We'd see it fluttering around, trying to get out a window, wouldn't we?" she asked. I agreed.

I searched the living room and kitchen, but nothing was stirring. Feeling mystified, I reopened all the doors and settled down again to the football game. Within a few minutes, Buffy went "on point," to the extent a cocker can go on point. He had his nose down, snorting excitedly, and his stubby tail wagged like crazy. There was something between the loveseat and the end table.

Sure enough, a junco skittered out across the room and under the davenport. About the size of a house sparrow, the junco's slate gray body has a hooded appearance, and its tummy looks like it's been dipped in a shallow tray of white paint. There's a definite demarcation between the gray and the white. White outer tail feathers flash suddenly when it flies, perhaps to distract or confuse a pursuing predator.

I surmised that our junco had ducked into a shrub next to the front door, out of the hawk's way, but then popped out of hiding when I opened the door, and, in a panic, flew right into the house. I collared Buffy and enlisted Jean to barricade the pup in the back room as I shut all the doors for a second time. Thankfully, both cats were asleep elsewhere. I drew the blinds and window shades, darkening the room.

Then I opened the front door and storm door to give the bird a clear and brightly lit avenue of escape. Next I got a dishtowel and leaned over the back of the davenport. One frightened junco looked up at me with dark eyes that rival a field mouse's in beauty. I tried swishing the towel at the junco to persuade it to head toward the open door. Nope. It went under the couch, leaving behind just the tiniest dab of whitewash (forgivable nervousness on its part).

I had to move the davenport. The junco was frozen in place; I tossed the towel over the little guy, gently wrapped it up, and took it outside. Then I may have made a critical mistake: I released it right off the front porch. Off it flew to our Juneberry tree. The sharpie above in the maple swooped down, zigged and zagged, applied its air brakes, and chased the poor junco up over the roof of the house. A sharp-shinned hawk's powerful, short wings are designed for chasing birds and other prey through forests.

I ran to the back bedroom window to see if I could catch any more of the pursuit. All I saw were a couple of crows heading farther west, probably off to harass the hawk.

Back I went to the football game, but in less than an hour, Rodd called to point out a hawk in their mountain ash tree. It looked like the same one. I prefer to assume it came back so soon because it was still hungry and hadn't caught the junco after all. The sharpie sat in the mountain ash for quite a while. I was able to get a few photos. As

I watched, it opened its talons, balanced on the limb for a moment, leaned forward, and dropped toward our front sidewalk.

I stood up to see its target, but couldn't see the hawk . . . until I looked more to the right. It was perched on the edge of the birdbath, thinking about getting a drink. I moved as slowly as I could to get a better look. It seemed to watch my every move. Next it hopped off the birdbath, perched a moment in the rhododendron, and took off down the block to the south. So much for a quiet afternoon watching football.

If there's a next time, even though a raptor has to eat, I'll walk any would-be prey safely out of a hawk's line of sight before releasing it. After all, a hawk, a barking dog, and a monster that threw a cloth over it had already freaked out my little junco.

Even in a sub-zero Minnesota winter, it's still a jungle out there.

Wren House

They'll nest in a tin can, an old flower pot, a pigeon-hole in a roll-top desk, a half-empty bag of concrete mix, even in the pocket of a forgotten garden jacket.

House wrens are very inventive about nest sites. The wren house at our place wasn't meant to be a wren house at all. It was sold as a bluebird house, but could easily be modified to become a roosting shelter for chickadees to get out of the wintry blast at night.

Come springtime, I was surprised to see twigs sticking out the entrance hole. Was a wren trying to build a nest in the roosting box? It didn't look like a good choice. Sticks couldn't be piled very high before they'd block the entrance. I knew that the male starts the process by shoving sticks into a nesting cavity. His zeal persuaded me to reverse the front panel so the entrance hole was at the top and to take out the roosting pegs. I thought it would be great to have wrens nesting right in our backyard. The wren was ecstatic!

He soon began in earnest to stuff the house full of small sticks. He'd arrive with a stick crosswise in his bill, grab onto the edge of the hole and then turn his head, trying to poke one end into the nest box. The stick was usually too long, but he kept bumping and sliding the stick through his beak till he could aim the shorter end into the hole. He didn't just drop it into the house; he *carried* it in. I'm sure he was arranging the nest just the way he wanted.

After a few days, it looked like our nest box was filling up. Was he preparing a nest for a future mate, or was he just jamming sticks in there to keep another wren from using it? I got out the ladder and peeked in the entrance hole with a flashlight. The sticks were stacked toward the front of the house right up to the entrance, but there seemed to be a deep open space behind them. And, in fact, I learned that this is the way the wren usually builds its nest, with sticks in front which it crawls over to reach the nest cup behind them. All those sticks in the nest box may have been to divert any rainwater that might get in, letting it run down the sticks, thus avoiding the nest, which is like a house on stilts.

Before, during, and after getting the box filled with sticks, our wren spent nearly every free moment singing his little heart out. A wren's song is like tinkling water, a burbling warble, which rises in pitch and volume, and then falls at the end. It lasts just two or three seconds. Not too bad if that were all. But after only a brief pause, a wren will start right back up again. You can get ten to fifteen repetitions a *minute*. You really have to love that song, or you'll come to hate it.

When I'm with a group of birdwatchers in the spring, and we hear a house wren singing, I firmly warn them about putting up a wren house in their yard. They need to make sure they *really* enjoy that song, because they're going to be hearing it . . . *all* . . . *summer* . . . *long*. I've even seen a wren sing with a big green caterpillar clenched firmly in its beak. All that singing is intended to advertise his territory and to announce to any passing females that it's really a great spot to set up housekeeping.

As for our wren house, I didn't notice any takers. Only one wren went into it at a time, and I never saw a bird in the box while one was on the wire. During the first few days of July, I heard very little wren song and had very few wren sightings. I figured we'd have no wrens in our wren house that year, even though at least one of them had been working on it in the spring. Then, in the second week of July, I was startled to see a wren putting sticks into the house again. Where'd he been?

A few minutes later, he was perched on the telephone wire above the birdhouse, singing away with a fledgling beside him begging for food. The baby kept edging closer and closer to the adult, with its mouth wide open, fluttering its wings, but all the adult offered was song. The baby seemed to be saying, "That's pretty music, but I can't live on song alone. What happened to those juicy green caterpillars?"

Even though wrens didn't breed in our nest box, apparently a pair raised at least one youngster someplace nearby. Maybe in my neighbor's garden jacket.

European Invasion

New York businessman Eugene Scheifflin thought he had a "wonderful" idea back in 1890: How about bringing all sixty of the bird species mentioned in Shakespeare to America?

Thus, he released sixty European starlings in Central Park that year and forty more the next. I don't know how far he got with the other fifty-nine species, but those hundred starlings succeeded spectacularly. Estimates put today's starling population at over 200 million in North America. In fact, Scheifflin's act led directly to federal laws restricting introduction of other wild exotics.

In 1929, starlings made an inglorious entrance to Minnesota. Thomas S. Roberts, a preeminent naturalist and birdwatcher, reported that in southeastern Minnesota, two starlings repeatedly flew at a farmhouse window trying to get at a canary in a cage. Those two were the first starlings reported in Minnesota. Today they cover the state and are found even in the Boundary Waters Canoe Area wilderness on the Canadian border.

Although the European starling is a chubby black bird with a short tail, when flying it looks like a jet fighter with triangular backswept wings. It flies very directly and fast. A flock that changes direction suddenly can look like a school of fish being pursued. Starlings appear heavily speckled in the winter because the new feathers they've just grown have dots on the tips. As the feather tips wear, most of the dots disappear; by spring their body shows an iridescent blue-black sheen. Their bills also change from black in the winter to yellow in the spring.

You've probably noticed that starlings at your feeder tray tend to spread seed all over the place. That's because their bill pops open like a pair of scissors, seeming to scatter more seed than it gathers. Starlings have more highly developed protractor jaw muscles than most birds.

That reverse bill action is called "gaping." Gaping helps starlings find food in the soil. They forage by poking their closed bill into the dirt. Then they snap it open, prying soil and grass roots apart, hoping to expose hidden, winter-dormant grubs. They enjoy dining on beetle larvae, ants, and earthworms, too.

Starlings also are renowned mimics. I've read they can copy up to sixty different birdcalls, including those of the killdeer, meadowlark, house sparrow, robin, and crow, plus the sounds of dogs, cats, and machinery. They learn from each other and may continue to learn new songs and sounds throughout their lives. They can even mimic human speech. *Arnie the Darling Starling* is the true story about a rescued starling that lived with humans and learned to "talk" with his benefactors.

Although they often nest in roadside sign poles and such, starlings are frequently in competition with many of our native tree cavity nesters, such as woodpeckers, wood ducks, flickers, kestrels, tree swallows, purple martins, and bluebirds. And, because starlings are the earliest to nest in the spring, they get first pick of available cavities. Few native birds can stand the onslaught of a determined group of starlings for a nest site.

Starling eggs hatch in about twelve days. The parents start out keeping a tidy nest, carrying away the nestlings' fecal sacs, but as nestlings grow they produce excessively wet fecal matter. The adults quit the sanitation process, relying on the little ones to defecate out the opening at the edge of the nest hole. That doesn't always work very well, so by the end of the nesting period, the nest cavity becomes a sodden, swarming "pest-ridden compost," as one observer has noted. It's unfit for any other bird to use for the rest of the season.

The fledglings don't look like their parents. They're sleeker, gray on top, lighter gray on the underside, with a whitish throat and chin. The first time I saw a couple of these mousey looking birds chase a shiny black starling around the yard, I couldn't figure out what they were. It took some searching in field guides to get the answer.

As a successful invader, the European starling has a mixed record. On the one hand, it eats the larvae of lots of nasty beetles and moths; on the other, it competes with native cavity nesters, forcing them to lesser sites or to not nest at all. Starlings often roost by the thousands, and their roost sites can leave a mess of foul whitewash below.

What hath Eugene Scheifflin wrought? I doubt he had any idea they'd spread over the whole continent. European starlings are, however, both pretty and talented. Then, again, they haven't roosted in my yard, and they haven't tried to attack my canary.

Burdock Busting

While walking along a trail in the old Lilydale brick-yard down by the Mississippi one spring morning, I saw a black glob caught in a burdock plant, a weed with marble-sized burs that were the inspiration for those familiar hook and loop fasteners. The burs hook onto an animal or your jacket and get a free ride to a new location to scatter their seeds.

Who had thrown something into this burdock plant, I wondered? As I got closer, I could see it wasn't a glob, but a small, somewhat desiccated bat firmly stuck to the burs. It had probably chased a moth right into the burdock, unable to avoid the burs until it was too late. Once stuck, its effort to free itself had further entrapped it. And there it perished.

Then one day I got a call from a woman named Mary in St. Anthony Park, near my home in Lauderdale. She'd been leading a team of volunteers who were removing invasive plants when they came upon a bird caught in a clump of burdock. The trapped bird was already dead. Did I want to see it? She thought it was a gold-finch. I met Mary at her home a few mornings later. She had saved the stalk with its trapped bird. I chatted with her, took some pictures, and agreed it was an American goldfinch.

Mary called a few days later to say she'd taken the bird and stalk to the Minneapolis Parks and Recreation office, where she used to be the horticultural specialist. Folks there told her the bird was a ruby-crowned kinglet. I pulled myself up to my full height and, with a frosty huff in my voice, told her I thought they were wrong and that they should check a good field guide. How dare they doubt my identification? Me, the Birdman of Lauderdale!

Then I closely reviewed the photos I'd taken at her house. The bird *did* have a very narrow bill, not a wedge-shaped seed cruncher like a goldfinch. And the wing was grey like a kinglet, not black like a goldfinch. I was wrong! Heaven forfend! I called Mary immediately and apologized for being so cocksure of my identification. I told her I agreed: It was indeed a ruby-crowned kinglet, one of our smallest spring and fall migrants. This kinglet is about four inches long and nests in northern Minnesota. Oddly enough, it often hovers in the air like a hummingbird while it picks insects and spiders off tree limbs and leaves.

I decided to do some research into birds and burdock. I learned that many species of birds have been found caught in burdock, not only the ruby-crowned kinglet, but its close relative, the golden-crowned kinglet, too. In 1909, biologist James Needham photographed scores of golden-crowned kinglets "sticking to the tops of the clumps on the most exposed clusters of heads." He examined the burdock heads and found the seed-eating larvae of both a moth and the burdock weevil. He determined that most of the entrapped kinglets were young birds. Apparently, the larvae attracted the young birds, which were unaware of the dangers the burdock presented. They may have successfully ventured a snack in the past, but their luck didn't hold. I suspect a windy day would be a very dangerous time to try to feed on the insects on burdock.

Professor Todd Underwood of the Department of Zoology at the University of Winnipeg, Manitoba, Canada, read my story about burdock and birds when it appeared in *The Park Bugle*. He e-mailed some questions and then sent a copy of "Hummingbird Entanglements in Burdock," which he'd co-written for *The Canadian Field Naturalist*. Nine entrapments of ruby-throated hummingbirds were documented in August 1985 in Delta Marsh, south of Lake Manitoba. All of the birds were caught on fall migration, perhaps attracted by the lavender color of the flowers.

I never imagined there were plants hazardous to birds and animals, but burdock surely is. Mary offered some suggestions for getting rid of burdock. Burdock is a biennial. The first year it looks like rhubarb except the stems are a dull purple. The second year, it sends up a tall bloom stalk, multi-branched, with flowers that look like small lavender thistles.

When you see those lavender thistles, it's time to strike. Cut off the bloom stalk at ground level and dispose of it in the trash. But don't cut the bloom stalk before that lavender color appears because the plant will simply send up another stalk. Don't bother trying to dig up the plant. Its deep taproot will break, and it'll grow another plant.

I hope you're as convinced as I am about the need to get rid of burdock. Mary, the birds, and I all thank you in advance for your help as a Burdock Buster.

The Mourning Dove

I always considered the mourning dove a rather stupid, and stupid-looking, bird. I couldn't imagine such a tiny head could contain enough brains for a bird that large. It reminded me of a brontosaurus, all body, but not much noggin.

I wasn't alone in my view. Pete Dunne, author of several field guides as well as other books about birds, describes the mourning dove as a "teardrop with a tail or a pear on a stick" and "No other dove seems so overall plain, so microcephalic, so tine-tailed." Jean remembers visiting her aunt's farm as a child and waking up to the dove's mournful, "ooAAh cooo coo coo" call.

Over time, I've come to see they're unique in several ways. The mourning dove is one of the few birds that feeds "milk" to its young. Not the way a mammal does, and not that type of milk, but special pigeon milk that's produced in the bird's crop. The crop is an enlarged pocket of the upper esophagus, whose walls secrete a milky fluid that's rich in fat and protein. For the first few days after hatching, the young are fed exclusively on pigeon milk. The young bird inserts its beak into the corner of the parent's bill, and the adult regurgitates pigeon milk for the youngster. After the first few days, partially digested seeds or fruit are mixed in with the milk.

I've also noticed the way a dove drinks from a birdbath; it doesn't dip its head and then tilt it back to let the water trickle down its throat like other birds. A dove sucks water like a horse, without lifting its head. Most birds can't do that. Because mourning doves pant when they get too hot, they need lots of water. They can suck up three times their daily water requirement in less than a minute.

Mourning doves are also prolific. In warmer climates, they can produce up to six broods a year, usually two offspring per brood. Here, in Minnesota, they probably have two or three broods in a summer. They build a flimsy stick nest in a tree or bush, sometimes on a building ledge, but rarely right on the ground.

Both parents incubate the eggs for about two weeks. The female usually takes the day shift, the male the night. After hatching, both parents feed the young, producing that special, nutritional pigeon milk. Sometimes the female lays eggs for the next clutch while the young from the previous cycle are still in the nest. The young fledge in about fifteen days, but hang around to be fed by their parents for the next one to two weeks.

With such a robust reproduction rate, why aren't we knee-deep in mourning doves? Some blame hunting pressure. Dove hunters in North America harvest more than 20 million birds annually, exceeding the harvest of all other migratory game birds combined. As Duluth author, birder, and scientist Laura Erickson says, "Mourning doves are not much smaller than Cornish hens, and falcons and human hunters agree that their flavor is superb."

Even so, hunting isn't the major cause of mortality. Non-hunting mortality is estimated at four to five times the hunting figure. And doves have a lot of other predators, too. Raccoons, rat snakes, and other reptiles, as well as blue jays and crows, eat mourning dove eggs and young. Both fledglings and adults are prey for raptors, mammals (think roaming house cats), falcons, and accipiters, like sharp-shinned and Cooper's hawks.

Besides predators, mourning doves are subject to the vagaries of rough weather. Downpours can destroy their flimsy nests, dumping eggs or nestlings onto the ground. An early snow can cover the ground to a depth that makes feeding on seeds nearly impossible. That's when bird feeders can be a lifesaver for doves (and other seed eaters). Occasionally, you'll notice a dove with missing or abbreviated toes. Freezing winter weather takes its toll on those that try to stick it out till spring.

Mourning doves live an average of one year beyond their hatching year. Half to three-quarters of the population dies annually. So the birds you see this year may not be back next year.

I encourage you to join me in adopting a new attitude toward mourning doves, treating them with more regard and respect. They are, after all, unique creatures living rather tough lives.

Downy Woodpecker

One fall a few years ago, Jean and I were birding on Loon Lake north of Stillwater, Minnesota, when I spotted what appeared to be an unusual-looking downy woodpecker. The underside was buffy, definitely tan, not white like all the downies I'd seen in our yard and elsewhere.

I was quite surprised and looked it up in my Sibley guide when we got home. There it was: the Pacific subspecies of the downy woodpecker, buffy underside and all. How had that Pacific downy made it all the way to eastern Minnesota? What a find!

Over the years I looked for another specimen but never saw one until one day when I was on the phone with my birding friend Val Cunningham and a "Pacific" downy came to the feeder right outside my window.

"Wow!" I said. "Val, I've got a downy woodpecker right here with a buffy underside! Have you ever seen that?"

"You've probably got a juvenile," she replied, a bit too calmly for me. "They tend to have a buffy chest and belly." So much for my musing on the Pacific subspecies. In fact, when I'd checked my field guide, I'd failed to note that the Pacific subspecies has spots on its chest just inside the shoulder.

As is my wont, I decided to research the downy woodpecker and find out more about this regular year-round resident. I turned to Gary Ritchison's *Wild Bird Guides: Downy Woodpecker*, a rich resource with lots of downy photos, including juveniles with buffy bellies. The downy woodpecker is the smallest woodpecker in North America, around six inches long, weighing just about an ounce. Both sexes are black and white with a white stripe down the middle of the back. A red patch at the back of the head distinguishes the male. The downy is often confused with its relative, the hairy woodpecker, which is patterned very much the same. If the two birds are near each other, you can easily see that the hairy is much larger.

If you see just a single black and white woodpecker, which one is it? With binoculars, or up close, the rule of thumb is that the downy's bill is about the same length as the distance from the base of the bill to the eye. The hairy's bill is longer than that. In fact, the hairy's bill is nearly as long as its head.

Like most woodpecker heads, the downy's is uniquely designed to handle the shocks it endures when pounding on a limb or the trunk of a tree. Plates in the woodpecker's skull direct much of the shock to the lower part and back of the head and to the neck, relieving some of the stress on the brain. The skull also has very little cerebrospinal fluid around the brain, which reduces the amount the brain rebounds on each stroke.

Like all birds, downies have two eyelids. The second eyelid, called a nictitating membrane, comes across the eye from the corner near the beak. When I started birdwatching, I was fascinated to learn that woodpeckers have a third eyelid for protection during excavation. They even have feather tufts over each nostril to reduce the chance of chips flying in. The cells at the tip of the woodpecker's bill are arranged in such a way that the bill is self-sharpening. That's very useful because a woodpecker uses its bill to excavate several holes. The most important is the nest hole where it raises its family. Downies also excavate roosting holes to sleep in throughout the year.

The woodpecker's head design allows it to whack into bark to get at the larvae and beetles that make up the bulk of their diet. Once they've uncovered a larval tunnel, their specially designed tongue goes into action. Tiny barbs on the tip let it "harpoon" a wriggly larva. The base of the tongue attaches to a very long complex of bones that separates the tongue into two "forks" extending backward inside the skull. The forks curve around the base of and over the skull, finally coiling around each eye socket. This allows a long tongue to be stored in a woodpecker's head like a retractable tape measure. When the tongue is needed, it can extend well beyond the tip of the bill.

One winter I unexpectedly found a downy just above ground level among goldenrod stalks. In the spring, the female goldenrod gall-fly lays its egg in the goldenrod stem. The stem then forms a ball or "gall" around the larva, which grows and fattens all summer. I watched the downy hang onto the stem and peck away at the gall to extract the larva.

On your winter walks be sure to look down and across fields for downies perched on goldenrod stalks. Just don't call one a "Pacific" subspecies if it doesn't have those spots.

Blue Jays

Although it would be hard to believe there's anyone who doesn't know what a blue jay looks like, let me describe one just in case. Their blue color isn't a pigment in the feathers. Rather, it's caused by light being scattered through transparent, gas-filled cells in the feather "filaments" or barbs. If a blue jay's feathers were ground up, the result would be a gray-brown dust, no blue pigment at all. It's taken me a long time to accept this fact and has resulted in being teased by my more knowledgeable birding buddies.

That beautiful blue is augmented by some very interesting white and black spot patterns on a jay's back when its wings are folded. In fact, the spot pattern reminds me of those little QR (Quick Response) code squares we see in advertisements. I can imagine a clever researcher someday photographing blue jay spots and then writing a computer program to scan and identify individual birds that way. To the human eye, the male and female are indistinguishable, but who knows, a computer program might be able to differentiate them.

The blue jay is a large bird, about an inch longer than a robin. The jay gets its name from its loud call, a descending scream: *jaaaay*. But jays have many other calls including whistles, a watery *kerplunk* sound, and even imitations of other birds. I was out with my pup early one morning and heard the cry of a red-tailed hawk. I searched the sky in vain until I connected the call with a blue jay in the tree above me!

Blue jays are related to the crow, raven, and magpie, all birds that have more brains, I think, than a bird that size needs. They tend to get into mischief. And they often think more highly of themselves than they ought. When I'm out in the woods, I get the feeling that the jays think they own the place. Their raucous calls announce their arrival to check you out. Sometimes they will "mob" an owl or a house-cat or other predator, but quite often it seems they're just yelling at each other. If you follow the calls to see what they're upset about, most of the time you won't find anything. They're very social birds and, sometimes, that's all it is.

They're clever creatures, too. Folks who put out peanuts in the shell report that a jay will pick up a peanut, consider it for a moment, set it down, pick up another, and continue this process until it has found the heaviest peanut. Then it carries the peanut off, stashes it for later, and comes back to select the next heaviest. Pretty resourceful, I'd say.

Jays can also be very aggressive. One spring morning, I glanced out the kitchen window and saw a large lump of something in the yard under the feeders. It looked like feathers, but in an odd arrangement. It wasn't a bird. It was *two* birds—a pair of jays. I got my binocs and saw that each jay had a death grip on the other's beak with one of its talons. They were in a standoff. Whichever one let go would get a bill right in the face. I crept out carefully to try to photograph the combatants, but as I got closer, they must have figured I was more of a threat than they were to each other. They let go at the same time and flew off.

Their aggressive nature serves the species well in other ways, however. Jays will chase hawks and owls out of their territory when they threaten the jays' eggs or nestlings. On the other hand, jays aren't above snatching an egg or a hatchling from someone else's nest. They are opportunistic omnivores.

Blue jays are generally permanent residents in their territory, but some portion of the population migrates, especially if food becomes scarce. They often migrate in silence, surprisingly enough, in long, narrow flocks that can number up to a hundred birds. In the nesting season, they're also uncharacteristically quiet, even secretive, moving with caution so as to not reveal their nest site to a potential predator. If they're successful with their brood, look forward to another four or five young blue jays joining their parents, aunts, and uncles in some family screech-fests.

Oh, joy!

"Them Damn Gackles!"

Over the years, I've tended to tolerate the few common grackles that appear at my feeders. But a recent year was different. Some mornings we had seventy grackles in our yard at one time, and once we had a hundred.

On those mornings, several fights broke out over a few pecks at the suet feeder, while a mob of "scavengers" on the ground caught all the chunks that fell. Meanwhile, over on the platform feeder, a dozen or more shouldered each other out of the way and displayed a lot of attitude. I really like birds, but grackles are so aggressive, gluttonous, and rude . . . they're hard to like. So, as usual, I decided to do a little research to see if I could find any reason to like them more.

Adult male common grackles are about a foot long with iridescent black feathers. Females show more brown plumage. Juveniles are brownest of all—brown plumage, brown eyes, and brown feet. Adults have yellow eyes that seem to glower under furrowed brows. Grackles often feed on the ground, walking, not hopping. Like starlings, they use their bills to uncover food. In flight, they tend to fly with steady wing beats in an even line, not undulating like red-winged blackbirds.

Grackles show most of their attitude in the spring when one male encounters another. They pose with their bills pointed straight up and their body feathers all puffed, really strutting their stuff, trying to look as big and mean as possible. Two or more of these guys will be posturing at each other at the feeder, while all the others help themselves to seed. "Keep it up guys! More seed for us!"

Grackles are well designed for seed eating. They have a horny projection inside their beaks, at the back of the upper mandible, like a keel extending downward toward the tongue. This sharp keel helps them to crack open seeds. They also use it to "saw" acorns, scoring around the shell and then splitting them with their strong beak muscles.

Like many bird species, grackles use their bills for something called "anting." They pick up ants and rub them under their wings and on their body, using the ant's formic acid to control the mites that afflict them. But grackles take anting to a new level. Grackles have been seen rubbing themselves with walnut juice, lemons and limes, marigold blossoms, mothballs, and even choke cherries. Sounds almost like a marinade, doesn't it?

In the course of my studies, I found grackles have a few positive qualities. They like to eat ragweed and smartweed seeds, which reduces the spread of these weeds. They eat beetles, grasshoppers, crickets, cutworms, caterpillars, and lawn grubs like those of the Japanese beetle. In fact, I once saw a grackle pick an adult Japanese beetle out of the air and munch it down. Hooray! On the down side, they also eat beneficial bees. Grackles often chase robins and steal worms from them. Grackles are listed as a major predator of robins, eating eggs and nestlings, and have been known to kill and consume adult birds.

There are more negatives. The common grackle is listed as one of the most significant agricultural pest species in North America, causing millions of dollars in damage to sprouting corn. Grackles peck at ears of corn while the kernels are still in the soft "milk" stage, taking just a few kernels from any one ear, thus ruining the entire ear. They also pull up sprouted wheat plants. Other crops damaged include rice, other small grains, sunflowers, peanuts, blueberries, and sweet cherries. Even when they go to bed for the night, grackles can cause problems.

They're gregarious, maybe too gregarious. Their winter roosts in southern and eastern states can easily reach a million birds, and include red-winged blackbirds, cowbirds, and starlings. One roost was estimated at over 10 million birds. That's a lot of squawking and a lot of bird poop mess.

Where do I wind up in my assessment of the common grackle? It's mixed, leaning toward the negative. Several years ago, a few of us were standing on a street corner in West St. Paul during the Christmas Bird Count when an elderly man approached and began talking with us about birds. He said he fed birds in his yard, but couldn't stand "them damn gackles!"

Since then, more often than not, they've been "gackles" to me.

Hunters

One morning I was out in the front yard watching Buffy when I heard a resounding "whack" on the roof of the platform feeder behind me. A bird dove over my head and swooped up into our neighbor's oak tree. It was a Cooper's hawk. Like the sharp-shinned hawk and other members of the accipiter family, the Cooper's feeds mainly on other birds. The word "accipiter" comes from a Latin verb meaning "to seize." The writer Pliny used it to refer to the hunting habits of a species of hawk.

This particular Cooper's hawk must have had a target on the feeder. Maybe in the past it had been lucky at startling some bird into flight with a strike out of the blue. As someone who likes to feed and watch birds, I experience a certain amount of *angst* to think of a hawk using my yard as a place to find victims. To me, the Cooper's hawk, like its relatives, looks to be all business. It usually hunts from a perch and appears to glare at its prey from under its heavy brow.

Another hawk, the sharp-shinned, or sharpie, is an almost identical accipiter, but smaller at nine to thirteen inches in length. At a glance, the two species look almost the same. One of my field guides compares the Cooper's hawk's body size to that of a crow and the sharpie's to that of a robin or pigeon. Both are gray with rusty stripes across their breasts. Cooper's hawks tend to take larger birds as prey, including mourning doves, woodpeckers, robins, pigeons, blue jays, flickers, and starlings, as well as the occasional chipmunk.

Sharpies prey on smaller birds and mammals, sometimes even dragonflies and moths.

Once during a break from writing, Buffy and I were out in the alley when a Cooper's gave us a start. It appeared out of nowhere, zooming down right toward us below eye level. After executing a smooth right turn, it zoomed between the houses, directly to our front yard feeders. Cooper's often utilize a stealth attack, popping out suddenly from behind cover to surprise their prey. I hurried out front just as it flew up from our yard to the neighbor's tree. I saw no evidence of a kill on the ground and the hawk's talons were empty. Looked like a miss. This was just the first of a series of attempted hawk attacks in our front yard while I was working.

A day or so later, a bold Cooper's swooped down and landed on the wooden patio table out front. It stood ramrod tall surveying the area and then stalked across the tabletop to get a better look at the shrubs next to the house. It was quite impressive, marching upright, with a focused stare. It apparently didn't see anything, or nothing moved anyway; it took off, and sailed across the street, again at no more than four feet off the ground.

Within another day or two, a juvenile sharp-shinned hawk used the patio table for the same survey, but then hopped off to walk around the patio for a closer look. It even crouched down and crawled under a low-spreading Russian cypress, perhaps looking for the chipmunk that usually hides in there. Then it flew to the base of a large Korean boxwood and looked up into its branches as if daring any of the house sparrows hiding there to make a move. None did. This young sharpie made another walking tour of the patio, tried the boxwood again, and disappeared. He was a very assertive hunter.

A few days later, Jean was sitting and reading at the kitchen table when a sharpie nailed a white-breasted nuthatch on a feeder just two feet from the kitchen window! It took its prey, flew to the roof of the platform feeder, stopped there for a moment, and then headed out.

Jean fretted that she should have tried to rescue the nuthatch, but I don't think her running into the yard would have changed the outcome. It was clear the bird-hunters had decided our feeders were a good source of prey. The accipiters had a one-in-four success rate. I just hoped the smaller birds would be ever vigilant and able to beat the odds.

House Finches

Singing got them into trouble. Well, not really into trouble, but their beautiful music led some people to keep them as pets. And that led to the species spreading across the eastern United States. I'm talking about the house finch. Its song is a long, warbled collection of short notes that lasts about three seconds and often ends with an upward or downward slur.

At one time house finches were native to the western United States and Mexico, where they thrived in the hot, dry habitat and in the lower elevations of mountain ranges. In the 1930s, despite federal laws prohibiting the capture and sale of migratory birds, some house finches were captured, caged, and brought east, where they were sold in pet stores as "Hollywood finches." In 1939, as law enforcement began to investigate pet stores selling these finches on Long Island, New York, one store owner opened the cage doors and set twenty of them free.

What's a western bird supposed to do in New York City? Flourish, that's what! Within a few years, house finches were discovered nesting in the city proper. From there, they gradually spread west, north, and south until their range now covers nearly the entire United States. They've done very well since their unceremonious release on Long Island.

In spite of their proven adaptive skills, house finches did suffer a setback in their territorial expansion when they began to contract mycoplasmal conjunctivitis in the winter of 1993–1994. The disease is a serious respiratory infection that can kill the bird outright. But even a mild case results in swollen, crusty eyes that can impede a finch's ability to find food and escape predators. The epidemic seems to have leveled out now, with only about five to ten percent of the eastern population affected.

Back in December of 1990, before they became widespread in Minnesota, a house finch was identified at a bird feeder in St. Paul's Highland Park neighborhood. The sighting was so remarkable it was posted on the Minnesota Ornithologists' Union website. Birders all over the Twin Cities Metro area called each other excitedly to make sure they'd heard the news. That day I was participating in the St. Paul Audubon Christmas Bird Count; we made a very slow drive through the alley behind the house with the feeder to get a glimpse of this rare bird. We found it. My notes from the day indicate it was six below zero with a -51 degree wind chill!

The industrious little house finch is about the size of the ubiquitous English house sparrow. The longish tail has a shallow notch, shallower than most other finches. The male house finch has a reddish forehead and chest with distinct brown streaking along the sides and the stomach. It also shows a reddish rump when it flies off. The rest of the bird is brown. The female, by contrast, is very plain. She doesn't have any red on the head or chest and is gray-brown overall. Even the female's streaking looks somewhat blurred.

I really began to admire house finches when I learned from citizen science surveys that this bird was competing for nest sites with the invasive house sparrow—and winning! I usually see house finches in pairs at my feeders. They stay matched up year round, not just in the breeding season. They seem to be good parents. They're very responsive to their nestlings' and fledglings' begging. Most summers they raise multiple broods of four to six eggs each. The "house" part of their name comes from their being found around houses, where they may boldly use hanging plants or leftover Christmas wreaths as nest sites.

House finches are primarily vegetarians. The adults feed themselves and their young a diet of seeds, buds, flowers, berries, and leaves. This is rather uncommon in the bird world. Most birds feed insects and caterpillars to their youngsters to give them the protein that encourages rapid growth and development.

How the male house finch gets its red coloring is also interesting. No species of bird can innately create a red color in its feathers. In the house finch's case, it comes from carotene, a pigment found in some fruits and plants. Carotene can also produce yellow coloration, so the male can have more of an orange or yellow coloring, depending on available food choices. The depth of the color on the male indicates his ability to find such rich food sources. It's thought that female house finches prefer stronger colored males since it implies he'd be a good provider for her nestlings.

House finches have made a huge success of their forced relocation to the east coast, and thence to the rest of the continental United States. Their happy trilling always spells "Spring" to me.

Red-breasted Nuthatch

When a woodpecker makes a hole in a tree, it's the entrance to a nest chamber or cavity in the softer heartwood. Many birds, including nuthatches, often take over an abandoned woodpecker nest as their own. But why would a bird smear pitch around the entrance of its nest cavity?

When I first read about this, I thought of pitch as the black tar used for road repair. Reading further, I discovered it was balsam or spruce sap, and the red-breasted nuthatch is the artist. The female does most of this "decorating" around the entrance hole, carrying a droplet of sap on the tip of her beak. On successive trips, she smears it over every bit of exposed wood at the entrance, extending several inches out from the opening. Incredibly, they've even been seen to carry sap on a piece of bark and use it as a tool to "trowel" the sap onto the wood.

On one of my first field trips with the St. Paul Audubon Society, I spotted a nuthatch and called out, "Nuthatch!" One of the leaders of the trip expanded the identification to "white-breasted nuthatch." I thought that was pretty arrogant! If I had seen a robin and announced it, would he have corrected me with "American robin"?

Months later, I realized he was only helping us recognize and understand that we can see *both* white-breasted *and* red-breasted nuthatches here in Minnesota. Thanks to the leader of that introductory trip, I learned to distinguish the two birds and to look for a black stripe through the red-breasted nuthatch's eye from the beak to the back of the head. I also learned that the face is white above the stripe. This nuthatch also has a rusty red chest and tummy and is a bit smaller than the white-breasted.

Early one August, I was surprised to see a red-breasted nuthatch at our feeder eating a few safflower and sunflower seeds. Was this bird migrating? I left a message about what I thought was an unusual sighting on the Minnesota Ornithological Society's website. I hadn't seen a red-breasted nuthatch since mid-October a year earlier. The red-breasted nuthatch is a smaller, slightly modified edition of the white-breasted nuthatch. Both are rather chubby looking, appear to be neckless, have sharp, chisel-shaped bills, and are adept at crawling up and down tree trunks and limbs. Nuthatches can crawl headfirst down the trunk, whereas brown creepers don't and woodpeckers can't do so easily. So, if you see a bird crawling down a trunk, it's probably a nuthatch.

Both nuthatches habitually cache food, tucking away seeds and bits of suet under pieces of bark. The red-breasted often plugs the hole with a piece of bark. Nuthatches even cache seeds in the nooks and crannies of the pattern on stucco walls. Unlike crows and ravens, which cache food for a rainy day, nuthatches seem to cache it nearby for short-term retrieval as a quick snack before turning in for the night or as a handy breakfast boost the next morning. It's their version of fast-food, no further preparation needed. Red-breasted nuthatches feed mostly on conifer seeds. Loose flocks of them can often be seen feeding at the tips of balsams, pines, and spruce trees working to pry the seeds out of the pine cones.

Nuthatches are cavity nesters, using either abandoned woodpecker nests or excavating their own nests in dead or dying trees or storm-damaged stubs. This brings me back to the pitch-smeared entrance hole of the red-breasted nuthatch. I thought I had an innovative answer when I read that the red-breasted nuthatch flies directly into the nest hole to feed the hatchlings. I thought maybe the pitch made it easier for it to slip in without bruising itself. But then I remembered that pitch or pinesap is sticky and might actually be a problem for the bird. In fact, there is one report of a dead female red-breasted nuthatch found stuck to the sap in the entrance hole.

Through experiments in the wild, scientists have found that smearing sap around a nest's entrance hole deters squirrels from raiding it and significantly reduces the attractiveness of the nest site to house wrens. The red-breasted nuthatch may be trying to dissuade competitors and predators with the pitch around the opening. Its breeding range extends into Minnesota's northeastern forests and up into Canada, although it will sometimes nest as far south as the Twin Cities metropolitan area. In fact, after I posted my sighting on the MOU website, suggesting it was a migrant, a friend here in Lauderdale notified me that they'd had red-breasted nuthatches at their feeder year round for the last two years.

So, the red-breasted nuthatch I saw at my feeder might have been a Lauderdale resident, not a harbinger of a wave of red-breasted nuthatches yet to come. But when I see one of these little beauties in the fall, it always reminds me to keep an eye peeled for lots more to come in the winter. They are a joy!

Hummingbirds

I watched a lady take a shower one summer morning . . . out on our front lawn . . . under the sprinkler!

The lady was a ruby-throated hummingbird that had landed on the sedums out front just as the sprinkler rotated toward her. I expected her to zip out of there when the water hit, but she didn't. She sat there and seemed to enjoy the coolness on a day headed for ninety degrees.

This bathing incident occurred a few days after my return from a six-day birding trip to Ecuador. While we regularly see only the ruby-throated hummingbird in Minnesota, the Andes Mountains in northwestern Ecuador are home to more than fifty species of hummingbirds. I was fortunate enough to see thirty-four of them, twenty of which were new life birds for my list.

In the United States, we typically think of birds living in certain geographical ranges, north or south depending on the season. But hummingbirds in the Andes often live in ranges limited by altitude, up and down, and not so much north and south. They depend on the nectar in flowers, often specific species, and these often grow and bloom only in certain altitude ranges and only at certain times of the year. Migration of many birds in the tropics is therefore often a vertical migration to an altitude where food is available.

We saw one of the most impressive hummingbirds in Ecuador on the slopes of the Pichincha Volcano in the Yanacocha Reserve at an altitude of 11,500 feet. The sword-billed hummingbird amazed us. It has a five-inch body and a four-inch bill! When perched, it raises its bill nearly straight up, probably for balance so it doesn't take a nose-dive off the branch. As my buddy Bill said, "There's a bird that can't groom itself." Talk about not being able to scratch where you itch!

We stayed at a place called the Tandayapa Bird Lodge, near Mindo, west of Ecuador's capital, Quito. Tandayapa Lodge is situated at 5,700 feet above sea level. Its balcony featured half a dozen hummingbird feeders. We saw most of our hummingbirds there. One superstar was the booted racket-tail hummingbird. This little guy is just over four inches long, including a pair of tail feathers that have evolved as narrow "strings" ending in large blue-black rackets, which the male proudly displays as it flits and feeds. As if that weren't enough, this hummingbird, as the name suggests, also has some fabulous white puffy boots. So with its white boots and those iridescent racket tails, it's a gorgeous bird.

But for sheer spectacle, the rare and elusive empress brilliant took the prize. It was a five-inch beauty with a deeply forked tail and body feathers that reflected the sun in dazzling green beneath a flickering golden sheen. How rare is this bird? If you were to look on a birding map for this bird's range, you wouldn't find a gray shaded area marking its habitat. Instead, you would see just two small black dots west of Quito (where we were) and one dot on the border with Columbia.

Most tropical birds have names consisting of two or more words strung together, and hummingbird names are no exception. They're usually very descriptive. For example, we saw the white-whiskered, tawny-bellied, and stripe-throated hermits, small hummingbirds with decurved (downward curved) bills. Then there were the brown, green, and sparkling violet-ears, four-inch hummers with, you guessed it, violet ear patches that flared out when they confronted one another at the feeders. They looked like gill covers to me. Some names evoke magical fairy-like scenes: green-crowned woodnymph, shining sunbeam, gorgeted sunangel, Tyrian metaltail, rainbow-bearded thornbill, purple-throated woodstar, and buff-tailed coronet. There's even one called the purple-crowned fairy. I didn't see it, but others did.

As I mentioned, the ruby-throated hummingbird is the only regular we see in Minnesota. It nests in the metro area and farther north, with the northerly ones migrating through in the spring and fall. We also sometimes see other hummingbirds in Minnesota. A couple of vagrant, rare hummingbirds might hang out at someone's feeder into the cold winter months. I think of the calliope hummingbird that came to a feeder in south Minneapolis as winter arrived a few years ago. It was captured and was almost successfully flown to the southwestern United States on an airplane. Unfortunately, it died on the way to the airport. We also can get an occasional rufous hummingbird, a northwestern United States bird. A few stragglers will wander through Minnesota from time to time.

Personally, I'm thrilled to see even ruby-throated hummingbirds visit my yard. I look for the young males that don't yet have the full ruby gorget at the throat and the females with distinctive white tips on their tail feathers. Just watching them hover and feed in flight, reverse direction, and challenge one another and even larger birds is pretty exciting for this Minnesota birder. And it all takes place just 980 feet above sea level.

"So You Wanna Feed Birds"

Birds and Berries

I've found the choices Jean and I made when we landscaped our property have improved our chances of seeing birds and other wildlife "up close and personal" all year long.

We put a Juneberry, also known as a serviceberry, in our front yard, just beyond the kitchen window. This tree does well in partial shade and will reach twenty feet in height at maturity. White blossoms appear early in the spring before most of the leaves. Then, in June, appropriately enough, the berries appear. They start out white, turn pink, then red, and finally become a deep purple as they ripen. Birds love them. I can attest they're quite delicious. The ripest berries are at the tips of the smallest branches.

This leads to some acrobatics as birds try to get at them. The most successful avian approach I've seen is to find a stout branch below some overhanging purple fruit. These berries are usually the first to go. Some birds actually dive off their perch and try to snatch a tasty one in mid-air. I've even seen them fly right through the tree, grabbing one on the wing, and then land on a perch beyond.

We've watched baby robins in this tree try out their branch grabbing skills, fluttering to keep their balance. Adult robins and house finches are common visitors. One evening we watched five or six cedar waxwings eating. They looked like they'd bitten off more than they could swallow (they don't chew these). The berry fills the bill from gape to tip, but the waxwing tilts its head back and somehow opens its beak a little bit further, and "glomp," down it goes. You can see the bulge in its crop where the berry awaits further "processing." And we saw one take three berries like that in quick succession. Three Juneberries in its crop really changes the cedar waxwing's sleek profile.

The next morning we had a couple of young orioles chattering at each other and devouring berries as fast as they could. They looked like fledglings, still muted in color and not too sure of their flight equipment. They persuaded me to hang up the hummingbird/oriole feeder again so they'd have sugar water if they wanted it.

We have other plantings that attract birds. Hummingbirds come to the flowers of a scarlet-orange Dropmore honeysuckle vine growing over the arbor. A Virginia creeper has spread over half of the garage wall. For several years in a row, a migrating Connecticut warbler has stopped by in late September or early October to sample the creeper's berries. What a fine, unexpected "yard bird" he has been.

One spring a few years ago, I replaced a couple of cranberry bushes out front. The old ones never flowered or had any fruit, but the new ones flowered soon after planting. The birds really enjoy their fruit in the fall. It's well worth the trouble to replace dud plantings if you really want to have an "edible" landscape.

Some of our flowers, like the purple coneflower, attract butterflies in the back garden. And sedum "Autumn Joy" is described as a "butterfly landing pad."

You'll see more birds if you landscape for them. For those of us in northern climates, I recommend Carrol Henderson's *Landscaping for Wildlife.* He has suggestions for plantings, flowers, shrubs, trees, houses and water attractions for birds, mammals, and butterflies. It's a good reference work.

As you plan your fall projects, think ahead to spring, and think about landscaping for wildlife.

Birding at the Speed Limit

People often ask about a bird they've seen sitting on a light pole along the freeway. I always say, "I bet it was a red-tailed hawk." They can never prove me wrong because now they're miles past the bird or days past the incident. So, once again, I come across as the bird expert I'd like to be considered!

But the truth is when you see a large bird on a light pole in the upper Midwest or elsewhere, it's a pretty good bet it's a red-tailed hawk. I've seen them perched on light poles all over the Twin Cities and throughout the state, as well as along freeways in Florida, Texas, and in other locales.

Red-tailed hawks have adapted well to the spread of freeways into their habitat. Kempt freeway medians and ditches offer a great advantage for a raptor on the prowl for prey. To the unsuspecting rodent, scurrying about for food, the hawk looks like part of the scenery until it opens its wings, drops off the pole, and comes in, talons first.

"Note to self," the gopher says, "next time study the big brown lump above the pole more closely." If there is a next time. The gopher probably doesn't care whether the approaching talons belong to a red-tailed hawk, a kestrel, a crow, or a pigeon. It's not into bird iden- tification; its goal to remain alive. But you can learn to identify these common pole sitters, even at fifty-five miles per hour.

The back view of a red-tailed hawk will show a dark brown shape, rather upright in posture, with a possible V-shaped pattern of white spots on its back. You may see the reddish-brown or "rufous" colored tail showing between the wing tips. The front view will show a cream-colored body, often with a dark belly band, but not always. Red-tailed hawks can be seen kiting or soaring into the wind, looking as if they're tied to the end of a kite string. They conserve energy by trimming their wings to hover in place over something they're watching.

One challenge of hawk identification, especially of the red-tailed hawk, is the variability from individual to individual. There are dark morphs, light morphs, differences between juveniles and adults, and even differences in different regions of the United States. David Sibley, in his *The Sibley Guide to Birds,* has a two-page spread on the red-tailed hawk with thirty-nine illustrations showing these variations in both flying and perched birds.

The American kestrel is another pole sitter. Much smaller than the red-tailed hawk, it's often seen leaning way over to look intently for prey. It most often takes grasshoppers, dragonflies, small vertebrates, and small mammals. In fact, it's rumored that a feisty mouse can battle an attacking kestrel to a draw and escape with its life. Kestrels also kite, but often flutter their wings to maintain position.

The crow is a familiar pole sitter, as well. It usually sits hunched over and bobs its body up and down with each "caw." If it's cawing and bobbing, it's a crow. That said, crows doing their "hawk imitation" have fooled me. Occasionally they will soar and dive with their wings pulled back in a silhouette that looks very hawk-like. My contention is that they do this intentionally to spook each other, to scare off a rival, or just for the heck of it.

Rarely, however, am I fooled by a pigeon. Its pudgy body, small head, and preference for sitting in a small group on the arm of a pole are my first clues to its identity. In addition, when pigeons fly, they glide with their wings held in a pronounced V position that is diagnostic. Pigeons also perch on wires, sometimes in large groups. I've seen them almost exclusively on wires in certain parts of town. It must be a habit the whole flock picks up.

Other pole-sitting birds also perch on the wires along the road.

Kestrels are especially fond of perching on a power line or phone line and dropping from there to snatch their prey. Crows will occasionally sit on a wire, but they're rather heavy for that. I can recall only once seeing a red-tailed hawk on a wire, and it had a snake in its talons. My guess is that it landed on the wire only to adjust its catch before heading to a more secure perch.

A word to the wise: Remember the focus of driving is driving. Leave the practice of bird identification to your passengers, or pull off to the side of the road. But if you find yourself on a relatively open stretch of freeway and see a bird on a pole ahead, take a glance or two as you approach. See if you can distinguish a red-tailed hawk from a kestrel and not be fooled by a crow or a pigeon.

First and foremost, though, eyes on the road. I have to keep reminding myself as well.

Communal Roosting

Even when I'm out walking the dog, I keep an eye on the sky. When I see a flock of birds, I instinctively start counting individuals.

But I'd seldom seen so many crows heading in the same direction as on one late January afternoon. I estimated at least two hundred crows streamed over Buffy and me, all flying toward the southwest. I'd noticed small flocks of crows heading southwest over Lauderdale other times, but this was a new "outdoor record." Where were these flocks headed?

I think the answer is related to an experience we had during another January. Jean had an early morning eye check-up at a hospital in Minneapolis. We arrived about 7:15 a.m. when the sky was still dark and overcast with a slight glow from the city's lights, with a hint of dawn in the east. As we got out of the car, I noticed hundreds of crows rising up out of the trees in nearby Peavey Park. Just one crow gave a brief call. Most fanned out silently across the sky. We had found a communal roost site. They were heading out for the day in search of food.

Like herons and some other birds, crows are communal roosters. They gather by the thousands in the fall and winter to share the benefits of spending the night together. Peavey Park is due southwest of Lauderdale. I think that's where my afternoon crows planned to bed down for the night.

It's thought that crows choose a city location for their communal roosts for a couple of reasons. A city location near a hospital parking lot, for example, offers a night light for the flock. If the roost is attacked by a predator (the great horned owl is often the culprit), it's easy enough to leave your perch and get out of the way. But it's hard to see where you're going if it's pitch dark. And having a night light helps a crow find a branch to land on when returning after the attack.

Also, due to the heat island effect of the concrete, asphalt, and buildings, a city site offers warmth on a cold winter night. Buildings may provide some shelter from the wind, too. When crows roost, older individuals roost on the inner limbs of the roosting trees, with the youngsters on the outside. This way the elders gain additional protection from an invading predator. The older crows repay this courtesy in the morning by leading the younger crows to preferred foraging spots.

Crows often gather in noisy morning "coffee klatches" just as the sun hits the tops of the trees. They seem to be warming their dark bodies with the early rays before they get down to the serious business of finding food, probably discussing where they're going to go for the day. Then they head out in different directions in smaller groups, most likely extended family groups. These family groups are important for crows. Last year's juveniles often stay with their parents to help tend the next year's fledglings.

After individuals and extended family groups have spent the day foraging, they join other family groups in smaller, satellite pre-roost gatherings. There's much chattering and shifting of positions in the pre-roost trees. Then, perhaps based on sun angle, changes in temperature, or barometric pressure, or the eldest crow saying "Let's head for bed," they begin to fly off to the main communal roost for the night with extended family groups flying together.

I think I've solved the riddle of where these crows head when they fly over Lauderdale in the afternoon. But exactly where do they come from? I haven't worked that out yet. We could suppose that these crows come from due northeast of Lauderdale, but I doubt that's necessarily true. The old adage about "as the crow flies" being a straight line seems to hold for the Lauderdale-Peavey Park connection, but I'm not certain the flocks all start out due northeast of us.

I can imagine crows spending a winter day checking out trash bins around fast food places or looking for road kill. There are several potential foraging sites to the northeast of Lauderdale: restaurants and shopping centers along some major highways. Are families of crows picnicking at these spots?

I guess I've just given myself more mysteries to investigate. Where do our crows forage? And where are their pre-roost sites? That's another thing I love about birdwatching: There are always puzzles to solve.

So You Wanna Feed Birds

One day in a small store catering to bird lovers, I spotted a wooden roosting box made especially for chickadees to roost together on cold winter nights. I told the owner that I was thinking about making one myself.

"Ya know, I've never seen one of those guys who still had all his fingers," he said, referring to the fellows who make bird feeders and nest boxes for retail sales. "They're missing a tip here, a tip there. Or they have a slash right through their fingernail. If you do it long enough, that's what happens." I decided then and there to buy a roosting box and forego the thrill of making one with my meager set of hand tools.

I asked him what he told people who wanted to put up feeders for the first time. He told me he first asks what their yard is like. If it's open with no trees or shrubs, he tells them they probably won't get many birds. He encourages them to put in some plantings that will provide good cover near the feeder, or even a brush pile, until they can get things growing.

The owner also suggested that folks begin by feeding birds with a vertical tube feeder. This design stores feed in the tube and allows the birds to get at it through ports (metal ports work better and last longer). The tubes are usually a hard, clear plastic. Droll Yankee, Duncraft, and other manufacturers make several designs.

As soon as you put up a feeder, the squirrels in the neighborhood will consider it fair game. I've enclosed my tube feeder in a metal cage made to keep squirrels out, but which lets most birds in. Larger birds like cardinals or blue jays can't make it through the grid, but finches, chickadees, goldfinches, and even downy woodpeckers, have no problem.

I also have a platform feeder with a squirrel guard or baffle around the pole under the platform. Our squirrels still try to climb the pole, but when they get to the baffle, they are, in fact, baffled. One of our friends had a squirrel nibble away at the edge of the sheet metal baffle and eventually get past it. I imagine, though, the squirrel probably had some serious gastro-intestinal issues.

Another approach is to hang feeders from a "shepherd's crook" pole. Some poles have multiple arms that allow you to hang a variety of feeders. Again, a pole baffle might be necessary. Smearing the pole with silicone grease may sound like a good idea, but birds can get it on their feathers, and it's nearly impossible for them to remove. The grease may affect both their ability to fly and the insulation value of their feathers.

A suet feeder, either wooden, metal mesh, or a hanging bag design is another good feeder. Then there's the thistle feeder, a tube with very tiny holes or a bag made of very fine mesh that goldfinch bills can get into. There are a variety of window feeders that stick to glass with suction cups. They're really good for bringing birds in close so children can see them better.

If possible, it's great to set up a birdbath with heated water. Birds really are attracted to a source of water, especially in the winter. You'll find such baths in catalogs and bird stores, but they are a bit pricey if you want one that will last more than one year. And you'll need an outdoor electrical outlet. Some folks who feed birds advise putting a board across the bird bath in really cold weather so the birds can drink but not bathe, thus avoiding the danger of freezing in frigid air.

To a great extent, the seed you offer will determine the birds you attract. For example, cardinals like safflower seed and whole sunflower seed because they can crack them open with their strong beaks. And chickadees love them because they know how to peck them open, holding them in their tiny feet. But sparrows, goldfinches, house finches, and starlings don't like seeds in the shell. Bonus: Squirrels don't like safflower seed either! Nearly all birds like hulled sunflower seeds.

I prefer the sunflower seeds without shells, too, because there is a natural growth-inhibitor in the hulls that harms the grass under the feeder. You can find prepackaged seed mixes in many stores, but read the label to see what's included. The sequence of ingredients indicates which seeds make up the bulk of the mix.

Watch out for packages that include a lot of cracked corn, wheat, buckwheat, flax, red millet, or milo (milo winds up on the ground; birds don't like it). Look for packages with clear plastic so you can see the contents. Examine it for pieces of stem and stalk, empty hulls, even weed seed heads. You want to buy seed, not inedible scraps.

I buy safflower and large sunflower chunks in bulk and make my own seed mixture, half of each. I probably go through 200 pounds of seed during the winter. You could start with ten pounds of each from the bulk bins in a pet store or bird store. You can see the seed quality before you buy it. Store your seed in an airtight container in the garage or shed, not in the house. That way if moths hatch from the seed, they won't infest your home.

In addition to seed, you can offer peanuts, shelled or whole, cracked corn, and mealworms, live or roasted. One of my friends raises mealworms at home and draws in bluebirds, warblers, robins, and indigo buntings. I'm a little too squeamish to consider a worm ranch in my home (I think Jean would have issues, too).

Wild bird stores, hardware stores, and big box stores all stock feeders and seeds, although inventory and the knowledge of the staff will vary. The library and bookstores offer good resources, including *Wild about Birds* by Carrol L. Henderson and *101 Ways to Help Birds* by Laura Erickson. Henderson even describes how to make your own feeders, but consider that small store owner's advice and perhaps let a pro do the work. I love birds and may spend hundreds of dollars to feed them, but I'm not willing to sacrifice any fingers for them!

Water Features

Our neighbor Bill has a large property filled with gorgeous plants, trees, and shrubs. In the midst of it all, he has a small goldfish pond next to a small, screened summer shed. It's a lovely spot to sit and reflect, do some reading or journaling. And, apparently, some fishing.

Early one morning, he looked out his door to see what was going on in the world. A startled great blue heron next to the pond leapt into the air, made a tight, floppy circle among the maples and some flowering crabapple trees before clearing them and flying away. Somehow the great blue had spotted Bill's six foot oval of water from overhead and had dropped in to feast on his six rather large goldfish. Bill didn't bother to replenish the "food supply." He figured it would be a losing battle.

Birds are attracted to water. Most books about feeding birds include a section on providing them with water in bird baths or other water features. Birds can usually find enough food to meet their needs, but water is sometimes another matter. Bill's fish pond wouldn't necessarily be attractive to other, smaller birds because they prefer access to edges, shallow places, or, possibly, near where a waterfall drops into a pond.

One water feature used more often these days is a small, artificial flowing stream. A sloping area is cleared, lined with plastic and rock, and a pump installed to lift the water to the top of the slope. Many people report outstanding success attracting birds to such a miniature stream. In fact, Mark Alt, a past president of the Minnesota Ornithologists' Union, was entertained by an oriole family bodysurfing down the waterfall in his suburban Minnesota yard one July.

A less expensive and more common alternative is the birdbath. These are most effective if placed close to trees and shrubs so birds can dodge stray cats and have a place to groom their feathers. A shady location will slow the growth of algae, too.

Sally Roth's *The Backyard Bird Feeder's Bible* lists three important things to consider in providing water for birds: keep it shallow for the birds' safety; provide a rough surface on the bottom for sure footing; and, if possible, make it more attractive to birds with the sight and sound of running water.

One way to provide that sound, and make surface ripples which help birds to spot the water, is to put a water drip over the birdbath. This can be as simple as hanging a plastic jug above the birdbath and poking a small hole in the side of the jug. If the hole is a bit above the bottom of the jug, it will reduce clogging from debris. Water-drip devices are available at wild bird stores and in catalogs. Some of these are self-circulating. Others require a hookup to your garden hose. In the latter case, you'll need to situate the bath so it can overflow or drain into an unobtrusive place. This may work best with a bath placed on the ground.

Supplying water to birds in the winter is a challenge in Minnesota. At our house, we're fortunate to have an outdoor electrical outlet near the birdbath, which has a heating element built into it. Some designs use an electric light bulb in the stand under the birdbath to keep the water warm. But that may pose a hazard if water leaks down onto the light bulb. If you can't run an electrical cord to your birdbath, you could try putting out warm water into it and let the birds have a chance to use it before it begins to freeze. You'd probably have to be retired like me to have time to watch water freeze.

Birdbaths aren't always used just for drinking or bathing. Several of my neighbors have occasionally found dead baby birds, or parts thereof, in their birdbaths. I think the culprits are usually crows. Some birds wade into water, soak their chest feathers, and then fly back to the nest and let the babies slurp it off. Crows apparently don't do that. They soak their food in water and bring back a soppy mixture of food and water to their fledglings. So one unexpected, perhaps undesirable, side effect of having a birdbath can be dead baby birds and body parts soaking, especially in spring and early summer, when crow babies are being fed.

Bill told me that from time to time on his walks around the village, he'd noticed a school of some hundred goldfish in Walsh Lake, in the northeast corner of the neighborhood. One day they were gone. I'll bet that same great blue heron polished off a bunch of them either before or after visiting Bill's pond for an appetizer, or, maybe, dessert.

Where Our Birds Spend Winter

Those of us who feed birds in winter know that a number of summer species stay on through thick and thin. In Minnesota these include black-capped chickadees, blue jays, cardinals, white-breasted nuthatches, house finches, house sparrows, goldfinches, and at least four varieties of woodpecker: the downy, hairy, red-bellied, and pileated.

Actually, some of the birds we see in the winter aren't the same individuals we saw in summer, but migratory visitors who've come from farther north to spend winter in the Cities where it's relatively warmer and where there may be more food sources.

How about those we don't see in the winter? Where do our favorite yard birds go when the snow flies? Of course, they can't be truly called "our" birds. They're the birds we see in the summer, but they're somebody else's birds in the winter. Where do they winter? Let's cover some of the more recognizable yard birds and a few others.

Almost everybody knows the American robin. It's a member of the thrush family with a red breast and brown back, head, and wings. They frequently nest in our trees and shrubs, even atop porch lights. Not all robins fly south for the winter, however, so the old "With a worm in their mouth" camp song is inaccurate.

We have populations that overwinter here in the Twin Cities. For years, there's been a small population that hangs around the University of Minnesota St. Paul campus where the buildings provide a "microclimate" to shelter them from the wind and where they can forage for crabapples and other berries. One St. Paul Audubon Society Christmas Bird Count found at least six hundred and fifty robins in the median of Summit Avenue, feeding on hackberry trees! Those robins that do migrate head for the southern United States or Mexico. They often migrate in large flocks, looking for places with soft soil or good berry and fruit crops. They're one of the earliest returning migrants in the spring.

Most of us see a Baltimore oriole at least once during the summer. They're also robin-sized. The male has striking orange and black plumage. The female is more brown and yellow-orange. Orioles spend winter in Central and northern South America.

The ruby-throated hummingbird is a gem that comes to our nectar feeders and flowers during spring and fall migration and sometimes summers in the neighborhood. The hummingbirds from our area probably winter along the western Gulf coast and into Central America.

The chatty house wren is a summer bird, hopping in and out of brush piles and very willing to use the wren house in your yard. These little guys winter in the southern United States and in Mexico.

The red-winged blackbirds that are so vocal around our ponds and marshes from spring through summer migrate to the southern United States where they winter with resident red-winged blackbirds that stay there year round.

Some of us have been watching chimney swifts for a number of years. They look like flying cigars, black with no visible tail when in flight, and sweptback wings that flutter almost constantly. Until recently scientists didn't know where these birds wintered, then a wintering population was found along the Amazon River in Peru. They migrate all the way across the Gulf of Mexico, through Central America and down to Peru, northern Chile, and northwest Brazil, a journey of thousands of miles.

The Minnesota state bird, the common loon, isn't a bird we find in our back yards, but we're all excited to hear and see one. Loons migrate from our freshwater lakes to saltwater coastal areas. Many spend winter along the southern United States in the Gulf of Mexico (which has given us concern over effects of the British Petroleum oil spill on the wintering birds). Some winter along the Atlantic coast.

Another bird we see in the summer is the great blue heron. This bird stands in shallow water waiting for food to swim by, be it fish or frog. Many will stay as long as there's open water. When the freeze hits the Twin Cities, they winter along ice-free ponds, streams, or coastal areas, mostly in the southern United States or the Caribbean coast.

You'll also recognize the great egret in flight, a very large white bird that looks almost buoyant despite its size. They're waders, like the great blue heron. Both egrets and great blue herons have been found in Minnesota on Christmas Bird Counts. Egrets from Minnesota migrate down the Mississippi River to the southern United States and along the Gulf Coast down to Central America.

For migrating birds, migration is one of the deadliest times of their lives. It's estimated that nearly fifty percent of songbirds die on migration, falling victim to bad weather, power lines, windows, and prowling cats.

We really shouldn't think of them as heading for a balmy winter vacation. It's dangerous and exhausting for these beautiful creatures, and a matter of life and death. All the more reason to welcome them back in spring.

"Woodland Birds"

Woodcock Walk

On the night of the first full moon one May, I stood in a field listening intently for a timber-doodle. I wasn't alone. About thirty other birdwatchers joined me on a St. Paul Audubon Society field trip, ardently seeking a glance at an American woodcock, a bird so well camouflaged that even though its population is quite widely distributed, very few people have ever seen one.

As the moon climbed higher and the night grew darker on the grounds of the Army Training Site in Arden Hills, a northern suburb of St. Paul, we began to hear the *peent, peent* call of the male woodcock. It's a short, buzzy note that sounds a lot like a nighthawk, another nocturnal bird, but it comes from ground level, not from up in the air like the nighthawk's call.

The male makes the *peent* sound in hopes of impressing a female woodcock. When that sound stops, you know a male has taken to the sky to begin his bizarre and perilous courtship flight. He soars up from the ground in an ascending spiral, making a winnowing sound with his wing feathers. To me, it sounds like a kissing sound, about two "kisses" per second. Others have described it as a chirping, twittering sound.

When he reaches an altitude of some two or three hundred feet, he plunges straight down, flaring out at the last possible second, landing right back where he took off. And woodcocks do this after sunset, in the gathering dusk. Now, would that impress a female woodcock, or would she wonder if the male had a death wish?

In *A Sand County Almanac,* Aldo Leopold writes about the wood-cock's courtship flight in the section titled, "Sky Dance." After de-scribing the upward spiral and the downward plunge, he says, "The woodcock is a living refutation of the theory that the utility of a game bird is to serve as a target, or to pose gracefully on a slice of toast."

Then all of a sudden, the group I was with heard a strong *peent* off to our right. We focused our eyes through the gathering haze, strain-ing to see the woodcock leave the ground for his high flying act. The *peents* stopped, the kissing sounds started, but no one saw the bird. Then we saw one flying across the field, then two, heading to another display ground nearby. I was able to light up one with my spotlight, and we got a glimpse of an American woodcock flying away from us. For many in the group, it was a life bird, the first woodcock they'd ever seen.

I used to worry that shining a spotlight on these birds might tem-porarily blind them, which could be disastrous when they're diving headfirst toward earth. We'd find a woodcock with its beak stuck in the ground, blinking, and wondering "What happened?" But they don't show any evidence of being bothered by the light.

Soon we heard *peents* again, this time off to our left. Again we watched, but didn't see the climb. This time we got to see the end of the dive to the ground and found the bird sitting in the grasses not far away. I got the spotlight on it, and its yellow eyes glowed back at us. Everyone had a chance to see it and get a better look at its color and size.

The adult American woodcock is a pudgy bird with a big head and no visible neck. It's about eleven inches long, including a bill that makes up a quarter of that length. Its back is camouflaged with a broken brown dead-leaf pattern and the underside is buff-colored. That long beak has many nerve endings in the tip, which it uses to probe for earthworms. The upper bill also has muscles at the tip so it can open even when it's underground and grab a worm like a pair of tweezers. Because it feeds with its beak stuck in the ground, the woodcock's large eyes are set far back on its head and near the top.

It's an odd look, but the woodcock is able to watch for predators even while it's probing the ground. Its ear openings are below the eyes, the better to hear those squirmy worms. A woodcock can eat its weight in worms, almost half a pound in a night.

In all, we heard and saw five or six male woodcocks that night. When the *peents* had died down, one of the men in our group asked if the quiet meant they were done for the night.

"Well," I said, "all that *peenting,* spiraling, and diving were performed with a purpose in mind. Now the ones who did the best are accompanying their lady birds off to a quiet spot. Maybe we should be leaving." And so we did.

What Owls are Thinking

I started talking to owls twenty-five years ago when I learned to imitate the hoot of the barred owl in the rhythm of the phrase "Who cooks for you?" (*hoo, hoo, hoo, hooooo*). It was pretty exciting when an owl responded. And for the most part, they've been good about calling back. That is, until one time on a St. Paul Audubon weekend retreat in Frontenac, Minnesota, along the Mississippi River.

One Friday night in 2007, I led a group among the Civil War graves in the old Frontenac cemetery. A barred owl had been heard near the cemetery earlier in the evening. Our group got there about 9:30, an eerie time to be in a pitch-dark cemetery calling and listening for an owl. We tried calling with a digital recording. Getting no response, I tried my own vocal imitation of a barred owl. Still no owls responded. The fireflies, however, were spectacular, and we saw a satellite trace a path among the stars.

Saturday night we went a few miles down the highway to Hok-Si-La Park, a former Boy Scout camp, now a city park just north of Lake City. The park ranger met us in the parking lot, and we assured her that we weren't rowdy teenagers looking for a place to party. "Oh, you're looking for owls . . . you *have* to be quiet," she said. "Stay as long as you like."

We headed into a broad meadow, ringed with trees, and came to an area where we'd heard owls in the past. Again, pitch dark. And, again, nothing but fireflies.

Truth be told, we hadn't had very good luck finding owls for several years. I rationalized that we were calling them right in the middle of their nesting season. I've noticed that calls seem to be most effective when owls are defending territory or setting up housekeeping. They think one of our imitative calls is a rival owl and come to see who we are and where we're from. But by the time May rolls around, they've settled on territories, chosen mates, and are incubating their eggs. In some years, they already may be feeding little owlets. They really don't have time to chase around the woods looking to see who else is in town.

For several years prior to 2007, they responded. What changed? Well, perhaps there's less habitat and fewer owls. Perhaps there's been a loss of prey species due to residential development, agricultural practices, or competition from other predators. Several of us discussed the possibilities after our most recent unsuccessful outing. My friend, Paul, wondered about the tape recording I used. He suggested that the owls might have become accustomed to it after hearing it all these years.

The recording was probably made in the southern United States because you can hear chuck-will's-widows calling in the background. That's a southern version of our whippoorwill, another bird that can call its name all night long. Any discerning barred owl might well ponder, "Hm . . . chuck-will's-widows here in Minnesota . . . I don't think so. Must be that guy with the tape again."

What's worse is that when I made the tape I started recording from the source tape too soon, and I've got the narrator saying, "Barred Owl" in a deep baritone before the owl itself starts calling. I tell the folks in the owling group that's so the owls know who we're talking to.

We all joked, imagining two owls sitting next to each other on a limb in the dark and one nudging the other, "Listen now . . . the guy's gonna say, 'Barred owl.'"

Then I play the recording, and the guy says, "Barred owl," and the second owl turns to the first and says, "How did you know he was gonna say that? You're amazing!" Maybe the owls are just getting a kick out of my efforts, but have long since decided not to respond to such an obviously flawed imitation.

Those of us who've been leading owl walks for a few years regale the crowd with quips and puns. When you can't deliver owls or any other promised bird species, you've got to give people something for their money. (Although since it's free, I guess they're getting their money's worth!) If we hear a dog bark on the other side of the woods, I identify that as a "Barked Owl." I'm always rewarded with groans and moans all around. Or if a train whistles out in the night, I call out, "There's a Great Northern." More groans.

One year, a young man brought his fiancée along on the owl walk. He had gone on his first one with his folks ten years earlier. After the weekend was over, he told his mom, "Same lame jokes as ten years ago." I think it was just what he'd expected.

After the cemetery trip this year, one new birder in my car said, "You know, I'd come back again just for the humor."

That confirmed my philosophy that you can still have fun even if you don't find the birds. I guess I'll keep doing it till it's just not fun anymore. Knowing the group I bird with, that's going to be a long time.

Lucky Thrush

They say cats have nine lives; one little thrush I knew of had at least two. I first met the bird when my neighbor rang the doorbell. In her hand she held a white bakery bag, rolled closed at the top. "My cat just caught this bird," she said. "I think it's all right. I didn't see any blood."

I peeked into the bag. The bird was active. It looked like a Swainson's thrush. They migrate through here in the spring on their way to their nesting grounds in the Boundary Waters Canoe Area in far northern Minnesota. The Swainson's is related to the robin, also a thrush, but is smaller and gray-brown with prominent spots on its chest and a buffy eye-ring. I was concerned that the cat had broken the bird's tail feathers or pulled some out. Such damage can be deadly to a bird and, unfortunately, all too common.

In the July-August 2007 issue of *Audubon* a report on work by Wisconsin wildlife biologists Stanley Temple and John Coleman put America's cat population at sixty million in 1990. It's estimated that the average outdoor cat has up to twenty-eight kills per year. In rural Wisconsin alone, they estimated some two million free-ranging cats killed a *minimum* of nearly eight million birds, more likely as many as 219 million birds a year! The numbers can be debated, but the overall impact can't be denied—outdoor cats kill a lot of birds.

My neighbor swore she'd never have another outdoor cat after the two she has have gone off to that great litter box in the sky. I carefully put the bag and its fragile contents into a box and headed over to the Wildlife Rehabilitation Clinic in Roseville. Admission of the "patient" went without incident, and I was soon home again.

I sent an email to the clinic's Info Line with the date, bird species, and my name so they could let me know the status once they'd examined the bird. A few days later, I received an e-mail letting me know the bird was doing well, and they expected it eventually could be released.

The neighbor was concerned when Jean told her the news. "They wouldn't release it back here, would they?" she asked my wife. She didn't want to risk one of her cats taking another shot at it. No, Jean explained, they didn't have to release it where it was found, though they often do that if they can.

Two weeks after the bird had been admitted to the Rehab Center, my good friend Phil, the director of the Center, called. He'd seen the Swainson's thrush on the white board listing of those birds ready to be released by volunteers. He thought it looked like a pretty special bird and decided to pull its file and learn more about the circumstances that had brought it there. That's when he saw my name and gave me a call. Would I like to be involved in the bird's release? Well, of course I would!

Jean and I went to the Rehab Center on a Friday morning. Phil retrieved the bird's file and told us that it didn't appear to have any wounds or injuries and was active and responsive from the moment it was admitted. But after "cat exposure," as they call it, they prescribe antibiotics to fight off the possibility (read: probability) of infection. Cat bites are notoriously infectious.

Phil took us back to see the flight room where the thrush and other birds were exercising their wings and building up their muscles to return to the wild. We also got a tour of the avian nursery—tiny robin and northern flicker youngsters huddled in plastic margarine tubs, like surrogate nests, with their mouths ever open waiting for the volunteer to come by on her eternal rounds.

Phil said it's like washing windows on a skyscraper. Finish one side, you just move on to the next, round and round, squirting little shots of mashed up baby bird food into their gaping mouths. As they grow, they're moved to juvenile cages so they can socialize with their peers. They finally graduate to the flight room, where we watched a volunteer net the Swanson's thrush and put it into a small box.

Phil transferred the bird from the cardboard box to a pair of small plastic mesh baskets that looked like miniature laundry baskets clamped together top to top. Then he covered the basket arrangement with his sport coat to try to reduce the bird's stress. At the door, we substituted a towel for Phil's jacket, took the baskets, and headed up the path toward the neighboring Harriet Alexander Nature Center.

We set the baskets on the ground under a large pine tree and removed the towel. The bird began nervously hopping around in the baskets. I removed the upper basket, and it flew to a limb just over our heads. Jean was able to get a quick photo before it flew even higher to another tree and disappeared into the foliage. My last view was of trembling leaves as it hopped farther into the tree.

Although the Swainson's had had a two-week internment in the middle of its migration, I hoped it would be able to resume its trip and get up to the Boundary Waters. It would have stories to tell its buddies about escaping from a cat and all about the time it spent in recovery with the nice folks at the Wildlife Rehabilitation Center.

Woodpeckers in Winter

In the October 6, 1970, entry in her *Journal of Solitude,* the writer May Sarton noted that the trees around her New Hampshire home were losing their leaves. She rejoiced, "Soon everything here will be honed down to structure."

I'd like to describe for you some of the birds you'll see working their way up, down, over, and around those "structures" this winter. These are the nuthatches, the creepers, and, especially, the wood-peckers. They're all more visible after the leaves have fallen. My goal is to help you identify these critters even without your binoculars.

Starting with the smallest member of my winter group, consider the red-breasted nuthatch. We've always called it the *rose*-breasted nuthatch at my house, and when one visits our feeder Jean still calls it "Rosie." The more common white-breasted nuthatch is the larger cousin of the red-breasted. It's about six inches long, blue-gray above, and stark white below. (Bird are measured with the bird reclining on its back, tip of bill to tip of tail . . . you'll find that hard to do). It's a very pudgy bird. Both nuthatches spend the summer caching away seeds for winter, so, besides larvae and grubs, you'll see them pecking away at their seed stores under bark and in crevices.

The brown creeper's size falls between the nuthatches at about five inches. It's a secretive bird, and its coloration matches the tree bark. It usually moves upward on tree trunks and large limbs. Sharply pointed tail feathers give it a good ratcheting grip upward, but it may occasionally jump downward to study a certain patch of bark again. You'll most often notice the creeper as it flies from the upper region of one tree to the base of another to start its upward creep. Some creepers do winter over, but begin to watch for them as a sign of spring.

Now we get into the woodpeckers. The smallest in our area is the downy woodpecker. It's about half an inch longer than a house sparrow. The downy's back is a sharply patterned black and white with white on the back and on the tummy. The male has a red patch at the back of his head. The hairy woodpecker looks exactly like the downy but larger, just a bit smaller than a robin. Some birdwatchers contend that the call of the downy is "pick" and the call of the hairy is "peek." The memory aid is "short i sound, short bill; long e sound, long bill," but I'm not sure the birds have read the same memo.

Between the downy and the hairy in size is the yellow-bellied sapsucker. Be honest. Didn't you think that was a made-up name when you first heard it? The sapsucker is eight and a half inches long with a messy black and white barred back. There's a white patch running up and down the wing, when perched. That's unique among woodpeckers. Both male and female have a red crown, but the male also has a red throat. It gets its name from its practice of putting a ring of holes around a tree and feeding on both the sap and the insects caught in the sap.

Two more woodpeckers are about the same size as the hairy woodpecker, but much different in coloration. The red-bellied woodpecker is as big as the hairy woodpecker. Its back is barred with black and white stripes and it has a pale brown underside. The male has a red head stripe that starts at the base of its bill and goes right over the head to the nape. The female's red patch starts just back of its crown, also extending to the nape. The name "red-bellied" seemed a misnomer to me until I happened to be looking up at one in a decent wind and saw that the belly really was covered with downy red fluff.

The red-headed woodpecker is an infrequent visitor to the Twin Cities area, but spectacular when it does show up. It's also the size of the hairy, but features bold, solid color patterns. When it perches, the color sequence head to tail is red, black, and white. The head and neck are bright red. The wings are solid black on the upper part, solid white on the lower. It's a striking bird whether working a limb or in flight.

The superstar of the woodpecker family in Minnesota is the pileated. It's almost as big as a crow at nearly seventeen inches. It's a mostly all black bird with black and white striping on the face. This is the original "Woody Woodpecker" bird. Both male and female have a red cockade at the back of the head with the male's color going all the way to the bill and echoed in a red mustache stripe extending back from the bill. The underwings are mostly white in flight.

We in the metro area have another member of the woodpecker family, the northern flicker, but it usually doesn't spend the winter. During spring and fall migration, it's seen hunting ants on the ground. It's pretty good sized at a foot in length, with a brown and black barred back, a black patch below the neck (that looks like a collegiate V-necked sweater), a spotted belly, and a red crescent on nape of the neck. The male has a black mustache stripe. Both have a yellow underwing in flight.

Now, you need to get out there and spot some woodpeckers and others creeping up, down, and around those winter trees. You should be able to identify most of them without binoculars. And, if you find an ivory-billed woodpecker (until recently thought extinct since 1944), give me a call!

Mob Scenes

I really don't like crowds. I was reminded of this again when Jean and I attended a Minneapolis Youth Symphony concert at Orchestra Hall. Afterwards, the lobby was packed with parents reuniting with their young musicians and grandparents offering congratulations. Although that was a friendly crowd, there was enough bumping and jostling for me to breathe a big sigh of relief when we finally left the lobby.

One type of crowd I do enjoy, however, is any mob of squawking birds harassing a predator. Crows are especially good at spotting one and calling in their brethren from all over the neighborhood to mob the culprit. Watching and listening for crow mobs is a good way to find an owl, one of their favorite targets. Owls and crows are archenemies. Owls reportedly can pick off a roosting crow without disturbing those on either side of it. My theory is that crows mob owls during the day to prevent owls from getting the sleep they need to maraud at night.

Other birds that mob predators or intruders include blue jays, songbirds on breeding territory, and red-winged blackbirds, which will harass a person walking by their marsh. Kingbirds chase and attack hawks that approach their nesting grounds. I once saw a photo of a western kingbird riding the back of a red-tail and pecking away at its head. The hawk looked quite distressed and very sorry it ever got near the kingbird.

We still have much to learn about mobbing behavior, but it seems the primary purpose is to drive away the predator. It may also be a way to educate younger birds about what the raptor looks like and how to mob it without getting killed. There's definitely a mixture of fear and aggression in a group of mobbing birds. It's possible the mob assembles just to keep an eye on the predator. It's better to know where the threat is than to be surprised by it.

One morning, some friends and I witnessed a different kind of a mob. We were in the Crepeau Woods in the St. Paul suburb of Arden Hills when my friend Val noticed a dozen or more chickadees scolding in, out, and around a cluster of trees. They were joined by downy woodpeckers and white-breasted nuthatches. When chickadees scold, it's much more genteel than the raucous crows. It's more of a "chsh-chsh-chsh," but persistent, mad, and definitely a warning. We suspected an owl was nearby. I started scanning tree limbs, especially near the trunks, for a snoozing barred or great-horned owl. I wasn't seeing anything.

Then Val pointed to a cluster of tangled vines and leaves just above eye level. "There's an owl in there!" she exclaimed. It looked like some kind of nest from last year.

"What?" I thought, "An owl on a nest this time of year?" Not likely. I studied the clump through my binoculars. We were only about ten yards away, but I still couldn't see an owl.

"Not on the nest," Val said. She directed me down and to the left, below the clump.

There sat a saw-whet owl with what looked like a hat of tangled vines. Unless it opened its golden eyes, I could hardly tell it was there. But it was beautiful when you realized what you were seeing. You can hardly resist saying, "Aw, isn't that cute!"

The northern saw-whet owl's name comes from its endless "whoop-whoop-whoop" call that sounds like someone sharpening a saw blade. It's Minnesota's smallest owl, only eight inches in height. The saw-whet eats mostly rodents and insects, but will take an occasional small bird. Hunting at dawn and dusk, it spends the day snoozing on a perch or in a cavity. These owls are more often heard than seen. I've heard them in the northern latitudes, but in over twenty years of birdwatching I'd never seen one of the little rascals until I got this up-close view. It was an adult bird (both sexes look alike) with brown streaks down its cream-colored tummy, *sans* ear tufts, unlike the slightly larger screech owl. It looked fluffy, all puffed up. We couldn't see its feet.

Another birder in our group said he'd read that the saw-whet's usual defense is to sit perfectly still, hoping it won't be discovered. Val might not have spotted it if it hadn't opened its eyes. Because of Val's discovery, I was determined to pay close attention in the future to scolding chickadees. You have to scan the trees and clumps around them very carefully, but finding a mob of these little birds can lead to some great sightings.

It's a mob I've learned to love.

Brown-headed Cowbirds

When I began birding, I reflexively reviled brown-headed cowbirds whenever I heard or saw them. Cowbirds are brood parasites. That means they lay their eggs in other birds' nests, leaving the host birds to incubate and care for the nestlings. It seems sneaky to just drop an egg into another nest and burden the host parents with a new, big mouth to feed. For me, it raises difficult moral questions.

The male cowbird is black with a brown head, neck, and bib. The female is a non-descript gray. They're smaller than a robin, with a thick sparrow- or finch-like bill. Cowbirds range all over North America, save northern Canada. They often perch on a treetop, perhaps looking for nests they can invade. Their calls include a high-pitched, ascending whistle and a "glug-glug" flight call.

A female cowbird doesn't just lay her egg in an empty nest. The host bird would know it wasn't her own. The cowbird waits until there are host eggs in the nest, lays hers, and then often removes an egg from the nest to keep the count the same. The cowbird has to get her egg in there before the host starts incubating the eggs. Once the host mama is sitting on them, it would be difficult to slip an egg under her.

Cowbird eggs have a shorter incubation period than most host eggs. When the cowbird chick hatches, it may push the host bird's eggs or nestlings out of the nest. Any host nestlings that survive must compete with the cowbird chick's big begging beak, which usually gets most of the food. Some host birds simply abandon their nest and eggs, even their nestlings. But some host birds' line of defense is to build a new nest right over the offending cowbird egg.

Even so, the hosts have to be careful. Cowbirds monitor the nests they've parasitized to be sure their egg is being tended. If the egg has been ejected, a female will often lay another one. If she decides the nest isn't viable for her egg, she may destroy the host nest, eggs, nestlings, and all. While this may seem like "retaliatory mafia behavior," it's very likely that the cowbird has learned that the host parents will instinctively oblige her by building a brand new nest. And Madame Cowbird can begin the "egg drop" game all over again. Cowbirds are known to parasitize at least one hundred and thirty-two host species. As a birdwatcher, I'm concerned about the impact on songbirds like cardinals and warblers. I've seen a little five-inch chipping sparrow parent trying to stuff bugs into a big baby cowbird nearly twice its size.

Cowbirds got their name from following herds of bison on the American plains where they feasted on insects kicked up by the buffalo. In fact, they were first called buffalo birds. The theory is that because they were following a herd, they didn't have time to build a nest and worry about incubating the eggs. Thus, they just found a convenient nest (like a meadowlark's), dropped an egg, and kept up with the herd.

If a cowbird chick hatches and fledges in a host nest, is raised by host parents, and listens to host songs, why doesn't it imprint on the host species? Why doesn't a cowbird chick think it's a meadowlark, for example, when it grows up? It turns out that juvenile cowbirds have a very, very strong affinity for other juvenile cowbirds. Soon after fledging, they get together in huge flocks, forage together, roost together, and migrate together. They learn their identity from their peers in these large groups.

I wrestle with a moral dilemma when I see cowbirds: Is it right to hate them? Am I projecting my own ethical attitudes onto them? Are cowbirds just doing what comes naturally, trying to make a living? My answer seems to depend on my mood and what other birds might be nesting nearby. We've encouraged cowbirds with our agricultural and forestry practices. Land that has been grazed provides the short grass where cowbirds like to forage, and feedlots provide convenient feeding stations. Feedlots close to woodland edges are especially attractive to cowbirds, which like edges. Cutting roads through forests creates edge conditions. Cowbirds don't penetrate very far into large, unbroken tracts. More roads mean more edges and more potential cowbird habitat. Conversely, fewer roads mean fewer edges and less cowbird habitat.

Cowbirds are here to stay. They've evolved away from building their own nests, or have forgotten how to do it, and leave us to wrestle with the results and our own attitudes. If only they didn't pick on songbirds.

Chimney Swifts

When I first discovered chimney swifts in the Twin Cities, I was amazed. I don't know where I thought they were typically found—East Coast industrial cities maybe—but I never expected I'd see them over the Twin Cities, let alone over Lauderdale.

That was until I visited the Villa Maria Retreat and Conference Center near Frontenac, Minnesota, on the Mississippi. One of the regular events at the Villa is the return of the chimney swifts to the Villa chimney each night, just at dusk. Some years, hundreds of chimney swifts have roosted there. After seeing the swifts in Frontenac, their flittery flight and twittery chirp became familiar to me, and I realized I was seeing chimney swifts over downtown Minneapolis, downtown St. Paul, and even lovely little Lauderdale.

A chimney swift looks like a totally black flying cigar when silhouetted against the sky. Its body is about five inches long and is tapered front and back. The tail is usually tucked closed and not visible. The wings curve back from the body forming a scimitar-shaped crescent from wingtip to wingtip. Flight action is a very rapid fluttering, followed by occasional glides. Although its beak looks small when closed, the chimney swift's mouth or "gape" opens very wide. That allows it to take its meals on the wing, assisted by exceptional eyesight, great speed, and agility. Most of its food consists of insects less than a quarter inch long—mosquitoes, flies, gnats, and flying ants—so it needs to catch a lot of bugs to keep flying.

Two swifts fly as a synchronized pair in a unique bonding display, one behind the other. The trailing bird, thought to be the male, lifts its wings into a V and glides. The bond is completed when the lead bird also lifts her wings, gliding in the same way. They glide for a time in synchronized flight, like aerial figure skaters.

As the swift pair prepares for brooding, their saliva glands swell with sticky saliva, which they use to attach twigs and small sticks to the wall of their chimney. Their nest begins to arc out from the wall like a small woven basket, which they settle into from time to time to shape it correctly.

Birders used to joke that chimney swifts didn't exist before there were chimneys. They did, of course, but they were called American swifts in colonial America. Before there were chimneys, swifts probably roosted in hollow trees and caves. Today, besides those natural sites, swifts roost in building airshafts, in wells, and in outbuildings as well as chimneys. The female lays the first egg even before the nest is complete, with both parents adding twigs to the nest as incubation continues. The clutch size varies from two to seven eggs.

If the mating pair's saliva is so sticky, doesn't that interfere with bug catching? No, actually the parent collects bugs, mixes them with the saliva, and stashes the resulting "bug ball" in a special pocket in its throat. When it returns to the nest, the adult offers a little chunk of the tasty "gnat goo" to each hatchling, then gulps the rest down for itself.

Although there may be many swifts roosting in any one chimney, there's rarely more than one nesting pair per site. And they usually have exclusive possession of the lower third of the chimney. Personally, I wouldn't want to be at the bottom of a chimney with ten to perhaps a hundred birds roosting on the walls above me. But then, I'm not a swift.

Chimney swifts are very social birds. When the breeding pair in a chimney has its first egg in the nest, any swifts flying above will pause over the chimney to look down and chitter their congratulations. They really get excited each time a little hatchling appears. They're like aunts and uncles oohing and aahing behind a maternity ward's glass window.

I've never seen a chimney swift perch and used to think it was because they had weak feet. That's not true. In fact, swifts have very strong legs and feet, remarkable feet that allow them to cling to the inside of a chimney. They have three toes forward and one toe back, like most perching birds. But they can swivel the back toe forward, giving them four in the front, providing the extra clinging power they need for hanging onto a vertical surface.

Chimney swifts winter in eastern Peru's upper Amazon basin, completing an annual migration round trip of 10,000 miles. The life span is about four years with an annual mortality estimated at fifty percent. So approximately half of them don't survive the full migration trip in any given year. They return when there are enough flying insects to satisfy their appetites.

We usually see them in early May in Frontenac and by mid-May in Lauderdale. They can be seen all day long, but are especially active toward late afternoon. Since they fly so fast, it's hard to follow them with binoculars. I try, but seldom do I get more than a few seconds before they whiz out of my field of view.

Not a Shrike

My son Drew and I went north one January in search of owls. Although we found some, the real highlight of the trip was spotting a bush full of northern shrikes, aka "butcher birds." Another thing I didn't expect to experience, but which I did, was a lesson in humility.

Our destination was the Sax-Zim bog, named for two of the tiny towns that border the bog, not far from Duluth, Minnesota. Sax and Zim aren't really even towns, more like a few houses around a bar, gas station or café. A bog is a generally flat area composed mostly of sphagnum mats, springy to the foot in summer but frozen solid in winter. Bogs support a variety of sedges, as well as spruce and tamarack trees. Most birdwatching is done from the roadway.

The Sax-Zim is a broad area, about 250 square miles, which provides a wintering habitat favored by great gray and northern hawk owls. These owls aren't very common in the rest of the United States, so the bog draws birdwatchers from all over the country. Several guides lead tours of the Sax-Zim during the winter to help birders add these owl species to their life lists.

As we drove the back roads around and across the bog, we saw a lot of interesting birds, including Drew's first snow buntings. Black and white and about the size of a large sparrow, snow buntings fly in large flocks, swooping over the winter fields as a mass, turning rapidly in unison like a school of fish. It always leads me to ask, "How do they do that?"

We nearly ran over a common redpoll because it was sitting in the road. As we stopped to look at this sparrow-like bird with a red cap and black chin, one of the owl tour guides came roaring up and nearly hit the redpoll.

We rolled down our windows and chatted with each other.

"You fellas lookin' for owls?" he asked. "Seen any?"

We said we were, but hadn't.

"I've got some folks from Tennessee here in my car, and I promised them owls, but we haven't seen any yet." He then listed the roads he'd tried so far.

"Gotta deliver owls to my customers!" he said as he tore off, throwing gravel behind.

When the dust settled, I noticed a shrike in a bush on the other side of the road. A shrike is about the size of a slender robin, mostly gray with distinctive black and white markings on its wings and tail. Plus, it has a very distinctive black mask that starts at the beak and extends beyond where the ear would be. Shrikes are usually loners who hunt from a high, prominent perch, but as we watched, two more shrikes appeared in the same bush. I'd seen a shrike in the winter at the Harriet Alexander Nature Center back home, but I'd never seen more than one at a time, let alone three in one place.

And one of them was doing what I call "bush-whacking," beating its wings around the base of the bush as if it were trying to flush out a mouse or a vole. Since it was the dead of winter, I assumed it was hunting warm-blooded prey. You could say that no self-respecting insect would be caught dead in northern Minnesota in January, but self-respecting or not, it *would* be dead.

Shrikes are often spotted in flight by their habit of swooping up to a perch. They prefer an open habitat, meadow or farm field with short trees or fence posts that can be used as perches. The nickname "butcher bird" comes from the shrike's unique way of storing food by caching it for a later meal. The shrike impales its prey on a thorn, a spike of barbed wire, or perhaps by stuffing it into the crotch of a tree limb. This maneuver can be challenging because the shrike is basically designed to perch and doesn't have the talons like a raptor.

It does have a hooked bill, though, which is good for dispatching its prey, carrying it away, and tearing it into pieces.

The shrikes eventually headed on down the road, and so did we. Next we drove to Stone Lake Road, where the guide said they hadn't seen any owls. We were delighted by the sighting of a northern hawk owl about a half a mile off the main road.

These patient hunters typically spend the daylight hours sitting at the top of a spruce tree, watching for a rodent to make a false move. It's odd to see an owl that large on such a thin perch. We were pleased to find an owl and beat the hired guide. You take your victories where you can.

You also take your defeats when they come—*gracefully,* if you can. Later on I looked at some of the shrike photos. Something didn't seem quite right. The facial masks on my "shrikes" were too short. Another northern bird, the gray jay, has a black cap on the back of its head. That jay's black extends forward into the eye, but not all the way to the bill, like a shrike. And there is no black on the jay's wings or tail. Furthermore, unlike shrikes, jays often travel in small groups.

Hmm . . . my shrikes actually had been gray jays. I should have taken a closer look and not jumped to identifying it as the bird I wanted it to be.

Noted birdwatcher and author Joey Slinger has a saying for someone like me that day, I'm afraid: "He sees too much."

Fall Migration

When we think of fall migration, we usually think of it happening in the *fall.* You know, Canada geese, tundra swans, warblers, all the usual suspects. But there's much more going on in the realm of southerly migration well before the fall of the year.

For example, one July 25th, I made a visit to Walsh Lake near our home. In the past, I'd observed several kinds of swallows gathered there to feast on the many bugs the pond attracts. I saw a bird rather high over the pond and thought it was a tree swallow. I brought my binoculars up to my eyes and followed it in flight for a few moments. Like a tree swallow, it had a pure white underside, but the wings were larger and had a white streak on the top side. The head was pudgier than a swallow's, the beak more slender and pointed.

"Sandpiper," I thought. "A little guy." That would put it in the class of sandpipers known as peeps, one of my most difficult identification challenges. I watched it circle over the pond several times before it headed north and out of sight. I jotted down some field notes and looked up the bird in my Peterson guide when I returned home. I think it was a least sandpiper.

That reminded me that many shorebirds start returning south in July. Fall migration in the height of summer? I sure wasn't ready for fall. We Minnesotans earn our summers, however brief, by dint of enduring the winters. What was this bird doing returning south already?

Least sandpipers are among the earliest returning migrants. They nest in far northern North America from Labrador to James Bay in

Canada and all the way across to Alaska. Their babies are precocial, born fluffy, ready to run and find their own food. So I can imagine the parents spending a few weeks showing the kids the finer points of catching bugs and how to avoid arctic foxes and snowy owls. Then the folks kiss the youngsters goodbye and head south.

They've got a long way to go, wintering anywhere from coastal Oregon and Delaware all the way down to southern Brazil. The adults pass through Minnesota any time from late June to mid-July. The juveniles follow four weeks later, with the migratory route already programmed into their little birdy GPS's.

The sight of a migrating least sandpiper in July seemed like enough reminder of summer's brevity. Then five days later as we prepared for our summer vacation, I glanced out the kitchen window and saw a hummingbird chasing after a house finch. I suspended my last-minute packing, put together a sugar solution, and retrieved the hummingbird feeder from the garage. The hummingbirds were migrating, too. Had they no respect for our feelings? Jean and I weren't ready to think about fall.

Ruby-throated hummingbirds spend the summer throughout the eastern half of Minnesota, but I suspected that this guy was from *way* up north and heading south to where he planned to winter in the southern United States, Mexico, or Central America. He was another reminder that summer was ending before it had started.

There are many theories about what triggers migration in birds. In the spring, it's thought to be related to their bodies' preparation for mating, swelling of glands and the like, as well as clues from sun angle. Birds apparently have a built-in annual calendar as well as a daily clock. They can tell from the sun's angle and direction when to head north or south. So those least sandpipers must have been able to sense that the Arctic sun had passed the highest point in the sky, the summer solstice, and was beginning to drop down toward the horizon a little bit more each day.

As for me, I'll take any, and all the sun angle I can get. I want to enjoy all the summer days I can until the leaves drop and the snow flies. I don't like some bird's early exit reminding me how brief a Minnesota summer can be.

"Hawk on My Feeder"

A Fall Day on Hawk Ridge

Imagine for a moment that you're a red-tailed hawk. You've spent your summer in Canada feeding and, if you're lucky, breeding, and now you're migrating south for the winter. As you cross into Minnesota, you see before you the inland sea of Lake Superior. You can barely make out the far shore and, in the interest of conserving energy, you decide not to head straight across the lake. Instead, you instinctively turn right and follow the shoreline looking for an easier crossing. You're not alone.

Every year from September through December, tens of thousands of hawks, over a dozen different species, head south and are funneled over that massive inland sea to the west end of the lake. In fact, in September 2003 alone, over 106,000 hawks were counted passing over Hawk Ridge, the most western peak at the end of the ridge that runs along the north shore of Lake Superior. From there, the hawks can go around the lake instead of risking a long flight across it.

The road up to the Hawk Ridge overlook leads to a wide spot in a dirt road where folks gather to watch the drama. Huge boulders line the downhill edge of the overlook. The view is breathtaking. Lake Superior stretches in the distance, and Duluth's tree-covered east end looms below. Conditions on the overlook are rustic, even primitive. There is no running water. The port-a-potties are down the road. Just below the overlook itself, but still in view on the edge of another ridge, is an "owl on a stick" decoy to attract a passing raptor. Often, a sharp-shinned hawk will come in to take a glancing swipe at the owl.

That's when you can get a look at the top of a hawk, an opportunity you don't have frequently.

Hawks generally ride thermals, or air currents, caused by warm air expanding and rising. The air above Duluth doesn't begin to heat up until mid-morning, so we try to get to the Ridge by about ten. By the same token, as the day cools down, the thermals diminish and the hawks settle in for the night. That's usually by about three in the afternoon. A northwest to westerly wind seems to be about the best for hawk flights. The day following a strong storm is often good for hawk watching. Overcast days tend to bring the hawks lower, which offers better viewing.

In the fall and early winter of 2003 broad-winged hawks numbered over 160,000. Sharp-shinned hawks came in at a distant second at 10,000. Next were turkey vultures and American kestrels with about a thousand members each. Other birds sighted during most Septembers include osprey, bald eagles, northern harriers, Cooper's hawks, northern goshawks, red-tailed hawks, merlins, and peregrine falcons. It's been exciting to see peregrine falcon numbers increasing.

Broad-winged hawks are quite impressive in migration, especially in numbers. They conserve their energy by riding the rising thermals in a rotating cylindrical pattern called a kettle, soaring in an ascending spiral, hundreds, sometimes thousands, in one kettle. Then, as the thermal begins to decline, they head out from the top of the cylinder, gliding in a single file in search of the next thermal. That's the point where bird spotters have the greatest success in counting the number of broad-wings in the kettle.

Hawks migrate over Hawk Ridge until December, with the larger hawks arriving later in the year. October is usually a good month for big numbers of red-tailed hawks. Mid-October to mid-November is peak time for bald eagles, golden eagles, rough-legged hawks, and northern goshawks. Arrival time at the Ridge seems to be related to length of day, weather, food supply, and the hawks' own instinctive patterns.

Bring your binoculars and your spotting scope and tripod if you have one. You'll find there are many folks with scopes on the Ridge on weekends and most are very good about letting you take a look at an approaching raptor. It's difficult to track a migrating hawk with a spotting scope, but if you can find them at a distance, you can keep them in the field of view longer, and pick them out from farther off.

If the conditions aren't right for hawk migration, there are still plenty of other places to go birding in and around Duluth. There are ponds and mud flats just south of 40th Street West and US 35. Park Point can be very good. The Lester River and water treatment facility are east of the city. And you can always run up the coast to Two Harbors where the area around the harbors is good for birding.

On Minnesota Ornithologists' Union Weekend, the third weekend in September every year, there are lots of people and a few dogs up on the Ridge. On Saturday afternoon, resident experts give informal talks on raptors. Periodically, a volunteer brings out a hawk that was caught at the banding station just over the hill, so you can get a close look at one of these magnificent creatures. The Friends of Hawk Ridge have a raptor adoption program. For a contribution, you can have your photo taken with "your" hawk, get a certificate of adoption, a record of the leg band number, and have the opportunity to release the bird.

Besides the events on Hawk Ridge, there are evening talks on Friday and Saturday (at the University of Minnesota Duluth) and birding field trips in the Duluth area on Saturday and Sunday mornings. But you don't have to go to Hawk Ridge on MOU Weekend. There are volunteer interpreters on the Ridge every day from September 1 through October 31 and nearly always an official counter/spotter.

Hope to see you on the Ridge some fall.

Rainy Day Diversion

I saw some really great birds on one fun afternoon. They were hawks, eagles, owls, falcons, and a chicken. You may perhaps have guessed from the list (excluding the chicken) that I was visiting the University of Minnesota Raptor Center. I'll explain my theory on the chicken later.

As a rainy day diversion, Jean and I took our grandsons to the Raptor Center following a sleepover at our place. As we entered the Center, we were directed to a tour that was about to begin. Our guide Scott, a University of Minnesota senior majoring in Conservation and Wildlife Management, led us to the indoor exhibits featuring a bald eagle, a red-tailed hawk, and a turkey vulture. Then we headed down the hall for the outdoor portion of the tour. We found ourselves at the top of a timber stairway. There we saw some remarkable birds housed in a series of pens on either side of the steps.

In the largest enclosure sat a golden eagle, a bird named for the golden sheen on the back of its neck. I'd seen a few migrating over Hawk Ridge in the fall and several in mid-winter near Durand, Wisconsin, but this up close and personal view was dramatic. What a majestic creature.

The kids and we got to see both a male and a female American kestrel, one of the few raptors with color differences between sexes. The kestrel is our smallest falcon. They usually take on large insects, even dragonflies, vertebrates such as lizards, snakes, frogs, and salamanders, and smaller mammals. Occasionally they'll capture another bird.

One red-tailed hawk was extremely interesting. It was a Krider's red-tail, a light-morph form. When I first came upon one of these beautiful birds in southwestern Minnesota, I was stumped. It typically has a white head and white undersides without the usual red-tail belly band. Its tail color can range from pink to white with a rufous wash at the tip.

Another enclosure housed a young barn owl, which apparently had imprinted on humans as a youngster and would now become a teaching and training bird, never to be released to the wild. I've never seen a barn owl in nature. They used to be found somewhat frequently in far southern Minnesota, and one was seen in Dakota County a few years ago. But their numbers are in decline due to habitat loss as grasslands and farmland give way to suburbanization. Its year-round range in North America includes the west and east coasts and south central states. This white-faced owl gives a shrill, rasping hiss, which would probably set your hair on end in the middle of the night. (If, unlike me, you still have hair.)

We had to search one enclosure carefully to find a couple of eastern screech owls. They were hidden in plain sight. Other raptors in the outdoor exhibit included bald eagles, great horned owls, a barred owl, and peregrine falcons. About halfway through our tour, I noticed that as one of the grandkids came to each cage, he looked at the bird and murmured a quiet, "Hi." It seemed he was just being courteous. I found it touching.

After the tour of the outdoor pens, we returned indoors. Jean asked whether they had any saw-whet owls in treatment. Scott said they did and led us into one of the large open classrooms. There, on a table, sat a large wooden box on its side with the open end toward the center of the room. In the box, on a little arched perch, a tiny saw-whet owl sat staring at us. At Scott's request, we kept our distance, gave the owl a little more room, and stood watching the elfin creature. I was very glad Jean had asked. It's very rare to get a look at that diminutive beauty in the wild.

And that brings us to the chicken. It was in a cage on a table on the other side of the room. Scott let the boys feed it some cracked corn. I think the chicken's role was to be the subject of the song, "One of these Birds is not like the Other."

Just think of the ways in which a chicken is not like a raptor. It has heavy wing loading, high weight in ratio to small wings. The beak isn't designed for tearing flesh. The claws can scratch the ground but not grasp a prey. Definitely not a raptor profile.

Hawk on My Feeder

The Vikings' game went to commercial, so I went out to the kitchen to find a snack. I casually looked out the window to see if there were any birds on the feeder. I log them in my "Birds of Retirement" journal. Yikes! No birds, plural, but one big brown hawk sitting on the roof of my front yard bird feeder. The Vikings' game was forgotten.

A couple of squirrels cavorted around the base of the pole. I was hoping the hawk would dispatch one of them, but no such luck. I called to Jean to come see this unusual sight. Just the day before, I'd seen a hawk in our neighbor's tree, escorted by a couple of noisy crows announcing a raptor in the neighborhood.

This looked like the same hawk, which I had identified then as a red-tail. It was small for a red-tail and didn't really have a red tail, but an immature red-tail often has a barred tail, horizontal bands, before it attains real "red-tail-hood." It's not unusual to see a red-tail soaring over the highway through Lauderdale or a nearby golf course, but I'd never seen one on my bird feeder before.

As Jean and I watched, a woman in a white coat and cap walked by. "Oh-oh," I thought, "this will spook the bird."

The lady glanced at the yard then looked up to the top of the feeder and stopped. The bird didn't seem to notice. She turned slowly and continued her walk backwards, keeping an eye on the hawk. I like to think she thought, "Huh. He really is 'The Birdman of Lauderdale'."

Almost immediately upon seeing the bird, I grabbed my camera and started taking photos. The hawk gave us a back view for nearly a half hour. Then it lifted its tail and shot a stream of whitewash into our yard. I told Jean it was getting ready to take off. "He's lightening his load." It turned to face us, gave me one shot at a front photo and headed off over the house.

I posted an e-mail note on the MOU web server about the redtail on my feeder, and said I had photos if anyone was interested. My friend Julian asked for some, so I sent him a front and back view. Within a few hours, he responded with the opinion that this was a juvenile red-shouldered hawk, not a red-tailed.

I studied several guidebooks for identifying characteristics of the juvenile red-shouldered hawk and compared them to my photos. My back view photos showed the even bands across the tail. The last band, or terminal band, was broader than the rest. One book mentioned three light bands on the bottom part of the folded wing, but none of my photos showed that. There was a lot of wind that day, so the hawk may not have been able to maintain a guidebook-perfect pose. My one front view photo showed large, dark, diamond-shaped spots on the chest, matching the guidebook illustrations. I was beginning to think "red-shouldered hawk" myself. But why wasn't it a red-tailed hawk?

After checking field guides and reference books again, I learned that the red-shouldered hawk is the smaller of the two birds. The immature red-shouldered has heavy dark spots on the upper chest, not a clear chest like the red-tail. And red-tails usually have a streaky belly band, which this bird lacked. The two hawk species show a difference, also, in the width of the bands on the tail of the juvenile. This one's tail looked more like a red-shouldered hawk's tail. I was convinced Julian was correct: It was a juvenile red-shouldered hawk.

I felt a bit embarrassed. Here I'd exposed my ignorance to a statewide organization of birdwatchers. I updated my posting to the MOU website and admitted my mistaken identification. Even more people asked for photos once it was identified as a juvenile red-shouldered hawk! To me, this was a phenomenal yard bird, even better than a red-tailed hawk.

Birdwatching can be pleasantly humbling. Despite suffering another chip off my ego, I'd learned a lot more about the juvenile red-shouldered hawk. I'd also had a close look at it for a good long time and was able to take good photos for future reference.

Once again, I hope I'll be more careful about jumping to unfounded conclusions.

Accipiters

We've had a "bushwhacker" in our yard from time to time. That's a term used to describe the way a sharp-shinned hawk beats the shrubbery to flush out its prey.

One year a sharpie literally climbed down among the multiple red stems of our dogwood shrub, perhaps after a chipmunk in the leaf litter underneath. Another time a sharp-shinned was perched in the Juneberry tree as we came home. It flew across the front of the house, skimmed a couple of rhododendrons, perched on the porch rail for a moment, and ended up in the neighbor's mountain ash tree, watching our yard, well, like a hawk.

The sharp-shinned hawk is the smallest of the three accipiters (ak-SIP-ih-terz) we have in Minnesota, and, indeed, in all of North America. The next larger, and very similar in appearance, is the Cooper's hawk. The largest is the northern goshawk, seldom seen in the Twin Cities except in the deep of winter. Accipiters use a *flap-flap-glide* in open flight. They have short, square wings and long tails that enable them to fly through forests at high speed, dodging around tree trunks and limbs in pursuit of fast-moving prey. Their usual prey is other birds.

In a description of fall migration in the Upper Peninsula of Michigan, one author wrote that warblers and other small birds, after crossing Lake Superior, settled into small trees and brush to rest and feed. Then he noted that around three in the afternoon, a sharpie or Cooper's would come swooping through the shrubbery and make chutney out of those lovely warblers he'd been watching all day. Shocking, but nature isn't always pretty.

Here in the Twin Cities metro area, we put out feeders to draw birds to the seed. And, in turn, we draw birds to the birds. Sharpies and Cooper's hawks visit feeders to find a slow moving bird. If you see the small birds in your yard suddenly freeze in place, barely moving even their eyes, then look around for an accipiter in a nearby tree. The accipiter will often watch from a perch and then launch a surprise attack. Sometimes it will glide through, below tree branch level, and then do a quick turn onto an unsuspecting bird.

We've had a Cooper's hawk fly from around the side of our house, past the front yard feeders, down the block to our neighbor's feeders, and then turn the corner at the far end of the block to check out yet another yard full of feeders. While on such an ambush mission, the hawk covers that distance at a high rate of speed, effortlessly dodging the trees and buildings in its way.

Both sharp-shinned and Cooper's hawks have a blue-gray back, head, and upper wings. They have reddish-brown barring across the chest and stomach, and wide alternating dark and light bands on a long tail. Each has a white terminal band on the tip of the tail; the Cooper's has a wider band than the sharpie. In the spring, birds have feather wear that can make that white band hard to see. Sharp-shinned hawks have pencil-thin legs. The Cooper's legs are more robust. Cooper's have a dark cap and often show a bit of a peak at the back of the head, while the sharpie head and nape are more uniformly colored. The tail of the sharp-shinned hawk is normally square on the end; the Cooper's is rounded. But this isn't always a good differentiating field mark. Female sharpies often have rounded corners that might make one think Cooper's. Again, feather wear can affect the appearance of the tail.

The above attributes relate to adult accipiters. When it comes to juvenile birds, it's even more difficult to tell them apart. The juvenile sharp-shinned hawk has heavy dark brown streaking (vertical stripes) from the chin to the belly. The juvenile Cooper's hawk has fine dark brown streaking that thins out on the belly. These two accipiters do differ in size, but if they're not standing next to each other, it's hard to get a relative fix on that. I've read that bird banders, who sometimes have to restrain one bird while they process another, keep male sharpies in a pair of six ounce vegetable juice cans taped together. The female sharpie fits into a can from stacked potato chips. A Cooper's hawk takes a fruit punch can.

I snapped a photo of the hawk perched in our neighbor's tree and posted it on the MOU website to confirm my identification. I had several responses; most agreed it was a sharp-shinned hawk, not a Cooper's hawk. But some were pretty sure it was a Cooper's hawk. Many of these folks have seen a lot of accipiters.

If you see an accipiter doing some birdwatching of its own in your yard, study the head, the tail, the legs, then check your field guide for the best approximation.

And if you're still undecided, think about what size container you could stuff it into.

Falconry

Carol Johnson waited almost a year for the chance to have her own raptor. During one fall migration along the North Shore of Lake Superior, she managed to trap a first-year red-tailed hawk in a net. She named him "Erik."

Before trying to catch a bird, Carol had to pass a very detailed test, apply for state and federal licenses, and have her home and property inspected by a conservation officer to ensure that she was properly set up to care for a raptor. That allowed her to become an apprentice falconer. She could have one bird, a first-year red-tailed hawk or a kestrel to raise and keep into adulthood. Even falconers at the higher levels of general and master falconer are not allowed to take adult birds because it removes them from the breeding population. Carol and Erik would have to work with a sponsor, a general level falconer with more experience in the sport.

"Falconry is one of our most highly regulated sports," she told me. For example, when she flew her raptor to hunt for small prey, she needed a hunting license and was subject to the same regulations and seasons as firearm hunters.

Keeping a hawk is not for the faint of heart, nor for those who can't make a commitment. Carol and her husband converted a spare bedroom into a room for Erik, which meant removing all the furniture and covering the walls with plastic sheeting and the floors with newspapers. When hawks poop, they often spray it. The room had a bow perch, shaped like a rainbow, and other perches that Erik was able to reach on a long tether. He also had a bathing pan. He seemed to like socializing around the kitchen table, perched on the back of a chair outfitted with a rope wrap around the top of it.

Feeding Erik meant defrosting frozen quail and mice and cutting them into small pieces. It wasn't a task for the squeamish. Erik was well fed and was exercised daily. When weather allowed, he could fly in the back yard on a long line called a creance that gave him freedom to reach more distant perches.

My initial impression of falconry was that the falconer was imprisoning a "free spirit." Carol thought that, for the bird itself, it really provided a very healthy start to its first year or two of life. The raptor gets a good, balanced diet, exercise, and medical care when needed. And, Carol added, red-tails in the wild have a first year mortality rate of over fifty percent and twenty percent every year thereafter. It was an issue of trading freedom for security, she thought. I decided we have to be careful not to impose our human assumptions on the bird.

"Erik was not a pet," she said. "He didn't 'love' me." But Erik depended on Carol for food. "He saw me as the fridge."

That was the main approach to training him. Carol used a whistle to teach Erik to fly from a perch to her gloved hand, where he was rewarded with food. Soon, Erik began to associate coming to the sound of the whistle with a reward. She weighed him daily so his feeding program could be tailored to maintain his weight at the low end of the normal range. If a raptor gains too much weight, it loses interest in training or responding to the falconer's whistle or calls.

Training went on all winter, and he was flown free several times. One afternoon after I met her and Erik, Carol, her husband, and several other falconers met to fly their birds in free flight, to hunt in an open field near St. Paul's Midway Stadium. Typically, one bird at a time is flown, usually expected to perch in a nearby tree, while the human partners in the endeavor walk through the field to scare up prey. The raptor watches intently for motion in the grass then leaves its perch to pounce on the mouse, vole, or rabbit that's been flushed. That's how it was supposed to work, but things didn't go exactly as planned.

Shortly after Erik left Carol's gloved fist, a train came thundering by on the nearby tracks. It scared up a flock of pigeons that had been feeding near the track. Erik hadn't been around trains before. The train, its noise, the pigeons flushing, plus an unexpected wild red-tail joining him in the air, probably confused or distracted him.

He forgot his training and headed for parts unknown. He was still wearing his jesses or leg straps, which Carol used to handle him, but these were short enough not to get tangled in branches. They were leather and would rot off over time. Besides, Erik had figured out how to get them off if he wanted to.

A day or two after Erik's departure, I saw notice of the hawk's escape and offered to chauffeur Carol through the St. Paul campus of the University of Minnesota and the surrounding suburbs to look for Erik. We weren't successful. Carol was sure he'd do fine on his own. He was an accomplished hunter, surviving on his own before he was captured. Her plan had been to release Erik in April after his molting period was completed and after he'd been bulked up for migration, but Erik had other plans and "graduated" early from his falconry apprenticeship.

Carol looked forward to trying to capture another bird during the next fall migration. Having and training a raptor is a kind of spiritual experience, according to Carol. I could see that in the way she talked about it and about Erik and the months they spent together.

Erik had a great start to his life as a raptor. Then he got a chance to live it on his own. I look twice at every red-tailed hawk I see, searching for any trace of a leg strap.

Urban Red-tails

As I drive the freeways in the Twin Cities metro area, I often see a large bird sitting on top of a light pole, staring intently at the ground. It sometimes seems like a very casual, over-the-shoulder look.

This is a classic sit-and-wait predator. From the back it's usually dark brown with some lighter spots, often forming a V pattern. If it's facing me, I can usually see a dark band around the belly. In flight, you can see the rufous, reddish tail as the hawk turns in the sky. And the underside of the wings often shows dark "comma" or "parenthesis" marks out toward the wingtips.

These birds are usually identifiable as red-tailed hawks, the most common and widespread large hawk in North America. But be aware that the red-tail is one of the most variable hawks in coloration and markings. There are very dark varieties, very light varieties, and everything in between. That belly band, for example, isn't always there. In fact, *Birds of North America Online* notes that there are up to sixteen subspecies of red-tailed hawks. The red-tailed hawk is one of our largest raptors, averaging about nineteen inches in length with a wingspread of nearly *four* feet. It weighs about two and a half pounds; the female is larger because her body includes the organs needed to make eggs.

I usually see only one red-tail at a time, but during February each year I often see two on the same pole. They're probably a mated pair getting reacquainted with each other, doing some pair bonding before the breeding season sets in. Red-tails are generally monogamous and have been known to live up to twenty-one years, though rarely beyond seventeen. Red-tails build a sizable stick nest in the crotch of a large tree and lay two to three eggs in mid- to late March. Incubation lasts for a month. After hatching, the nestlings are fed chunks of rodents by both parents. The youngsters are ready to try flight after about six weeks, but remain with their folks for up to six months longer.

As I've noted, red-tails are classic sit-and-wait hunters. They watch for motion in the grasses and then drop and glide to pounce on unsuspecting prey. I got a call a year or so ago from a neighbor concerned that there was an injured hawk in a yard nearby. I went over to take a look. A red-tailed hawk was sprawled on the ground. It would sure look injured to most people. But this hawk was spreading out its wings and mantling, or covering, a meal of fresh-caught squirrel it was determined to protect from any other raptors in the area. And, sure enough, another red-tail was watching from a nearby tree.

Red-tails also hunt by soaring in circles above fields, using their telescopic vision to focus on a potential meal below. They feast on rodents, rabbits, pheasants, quail, even snakes. One hazard when catching a rodent or rabbit is the possibility of being bitten by your prey. Hawks have been found with bite marks on their toes and legs. It's especially a problem with younger hawks just learning how to dispatch critters quickly.

Another problem younger hawks encounter is harassment from crows. I used to have an office with windows overlooking the Minnesota River. Even if I couldn't see the barred pattern on the juvenile's tail, I could recognize younger red-tailed hawks because they let the crows get to them, diving down to get away, flapping out of the area. The more mature hawks just maintained course and speed and if a crow got too close, they flipped upside down and presented the nagging crow with an impressive set of talons. The crow usually abandoned its attack.

The red-tail's cry is a downward slurring "keer-r-r." It always gets me looking up, usually into the sun. But beware. It's a cry that can be imitated by a starling or a blue jay. I think they mimic a red-tail to eliminate the competition at the feeder by scaring the dickens out of other birds. Or maybe they do it just for the fun of it. If you hear that cry and don't see a red-tail, look for a nearby imitator, probably chuckling to itself.

"Dawn of the Lesser Sandhill Cranes"

Dipper Quest

I've always wanted to discover a new bird, one never before recorded in Minnesota, either an unexpected wanderer or a denizen of a secret habitat. I thought my opportunity had arrived when a canoeist reported what he thought was an American dipper in the Boundary Waters Canoe Area Wilderness in northern Minnesota.

A robin-sized bird, the dipper is found in the Rocky Mountains and Western states. It's endowed with longish legs and very long toes with sharp toenails that allow it to grasp slippery rocks in fast-flowing streams. It has the unusual habit of walking below the surface to pry nymphs, larvae, and other invertebrates from the rocks. It even uses its wings to "fly" underwater in order to catch crayfish and small fish.

I'd heard rumors for years that there might be dippers living in the fast-moving streams of northeastern Minnesota. I thought no one had actually seen one in the state. My theory was that the streams were too difficult to explore, or that people who had seen a dipper didn't know it was noteworthy. But I hadn't done my homework. In fact, American dippers had been reported in streams along the North Shore of Lake Superior in the 1970s. However, no sightings had been documented since then. The canoeist's report was in response to an article by Jim Williams in the Minneapolis *Star Tribune* about the dipper, urging visitors to keep an eye out for the bird.

Williams posted the canoeist's sighting on the Minnesota Ornithologists' Union electronic bulletin board. Randy Frederickson, a birder from Willmar, issued an invitation asking if anyone was interested in mounting an expedition to look for the dipper. I responded, and we began to plan our dipper quest. I was excited. Maybe I could still be part of documenting a confirmed sighting of an unusual bird in Minnesota.

Randy and I had never met, so we did our planning by e-mail and the occasional phone call. As the departure date approached, Randy asked me how old I was.

"I'm 66," I replied.

"Are you in pretty good shape?" he asked.

"No! I weigh over 200 pounds."

Randy, who was forty-eight, said, "Drat! I was hoping you'd haul my sorry butt across the portages."

The Dipper Quest got underway in late June. Our base was a cabin at Tuscarora Lodge, forty-seven miles up the Gunflint Trail from Grand Marais on Lake Superior, near our set-in point on the Cross River. We started out after a quick breakfast, paddling and portaging through several lakes to Cross Bay Lake, where the canoeist had reported the dipper in May.

The first portage was the longest, fifty rods or about eight hundred feet. But that doesn't do justice to the topography. It was up, down, through mud, up some more, and down to the next lake, with the usual assortment of tree roots and rocks to negotiate. Then there were two shorter portages with timbers retaining the soil on the climb up from the lake, but the "steps" sometimes had a rise of two feet. Not so bad for me, with a pack, paddles, and other miscellaneous gear, but Randy had the seventy-pound canoe on his back. Stepping up a "staircase" of two-foot high steps was no easy task for him.

As we reached Cross Bay Lake, a loon appeared near our canoe. The loon seemed to be in threat posture, head down and forward, looking right at us. As we glided past, it went into a shallow dive. I watched that beautiful black and white back come at me just below the surface, pass under the canoe, and reappear on the other side. What an incredible welcome to Cross Bay Lake.

We paddled to the south end of the lake where a stream comes in from Rib Lake and ends in a waterfall. The stream cascaded with a vigorous flow about ten feet over rock ledges and spanned some fifty feet. We spent a fair amount of time examining each rock, log, ledge, and ripple, looking for a sign of the blue-gray bird. No luck. Randy hiked the stream to look for a dipper or some likely habitat, a possible nest, or potential nest sites. I kept an eye on the falls, scanning them for another two hours. Neither of us saw a dipper.

A week before our trip, my brother Ed had given me a gag gift for my birthday. It was a blue-gray ladle. He told me it was a "dipper" in case we didn't see one up north. I showed it to Randy before we left home, and he insisted we take it with us.

We decided to call it a day in our search, but first we paddled up to the falls, propped the plastic dipper on a rock and took a couple photos. (So we could tell ourselves we got some pictures of a dipper, even if we didn't find the bird.) Then we retraced our route back across those same lakes and portages.

The next day we visited outfitters and lodges, handing out posters picturing the American dipper. We asked folks to contact Audubon Minnesota if they saw one. We also scouted possible locations for nest boxes, which dippers out West seem to adapt to very nicely. Not far from Tuscarora Lodge, along a snowmobile trail and spanning a rapids on the Cross River, we found a bridge that showed some potential for placing a nest box.

Randy predicted that I'd be back up north again soon, looking for the dipper. I haven't made it yet, but I hope he's right. I think of the quest every time I see that plastic dipper on my bookshelf.

Pelagic Journeys

I spent four days one late September and early October bobbing about on the Pacific Ocean with three of my birding buddies. We were participating on what are called pelagic trips. Each day we looked for birds that spend most of their lives out at sea, usually coming to shore only to breed.

Our first trip was out of Bodega Bay, north of San Francisco. The other three originated in Monterey Bay to the south. Each vessel was a forty-foot sport fishing boat with a small cabin, an open afterdeck, narrow side decks, and a small deck space at the bow. Thirty to forty birders made each trip.

After coming on board, everyone assembled on the afterdeck for an introductory lecture. Our captain and guide, Debi Shearwater, strongly encouraged us to take our seasickness medication if we hadn't already. "If you feel sick, move to the back rail of the boat as quickly as you can," she advised. "If you need assistance, we will help you get to the back rail. If you don't feel you need assistance, we will *still* help you to the back rail." Hurling your breakfast over the side rail would blow into other people's very unhappy faces. Not a pretty prospect. So, back rail it is, and if you're looking at birds, make room for someone with a green face charging back there.

My three friends and I snickered and joked that those hanging over the back rail would be chumming—feeding the fish and gulls. In fact, Debi had one of her crew do the chumming from time to time by tossing popcorn, crushed snack chips, and chunks of anchovy over the back rail, pulling a flock of squawking gulls along in the wake of the boat. Her theory was that this noisy flock would draw in the other birds we were looking for. She was right.

We saw a lot of great birds on our first day out. The most numerous were sooty shearwaters. A shearwater skims the surface. It looks like a boomerang with first one and then the other wing almost touching the water. Since you're watching from a moving boat across 500 or more feet of waves and swells, the bird slips into wave troughs from time to time and you lose sight of it. You have to guess whether you'll see it over the next wave, or if it will change course and head in the opposite direction, if it actually reappears. Like most seabirds, each of the four shearwater species we saw was a study in black and white, with the whiteness of underwing, belly, or both, helping to identify the bird.

Besides shearwaters, we saw albatrosses. The most common was the black-footed, a sooty-brown bird with a white rump patch and a seven-foot wingspan that also does the "shearwater skim" across the waves. It's impressive to see such a large bird skimming with a wingtip nearly in the water. First, the bird's back and the top of its wings are toward you. Then it flips and the underside of the bird and its wings sail by.

A number of birds harassed the gulls, trying to get them to regurgitate their food in order to steal it from them, a tough way to make a living and tough on the gulls, too, I'm sure. These "pirates" included South Polar skuas and three kinds of jaegers: pomarine, long-tailed, and parasitic.

The hardest birds to see and identify were the storm-petrels, small six to nine inch birds, with wingspans from fifteen to twenty-two inches. They're very dark and fly and flutter like bats or nighthawks, usually just below or at the horizon. We only got brief looks from a great distance. The tour guides can identify them by size and the way they fly, but a rookie like me just shouts, "Storm-petrel!" and leaves the identification to the experts.

I added seventeen birds to my life list on that first trip. With three more pelagic trips to go, I expected a bonanza of life birds by week's end. During our four trips we also saw a number of dolphins and hump-backed whales, but unfortunately not many birds on the other three days. I added just three more new birds to my list.

The sky on our last trip was clear and bright, but the swells reached twelve feet with a strong crosswind that made standing upright, let alone trying to look at a bird, challenging, and there weren't many to look at. Seawater washed across the afterdeck by the end of the trip. My buddy Bill and I sat in a booth in the cabin on that last trip. The boat pitched up and down and listed from side to side on the swells. We noticed a woman huddled against the window on a side bench. She was turning greener by the minute.

"I give her less than half an hour," whispered Bill.

Sure enough, she suddenly struggled to her feet, clapped her hand over her mouth, and headed to the cabin door. Her husband, who'd been checking on her, took her arm and shouted, "Mary's got to get through!"

And, by golly, Mary got through. The birders parted, she got to the back rail, and leaned over just in time. Her husband stood at her left side, gently rubbing her back with his right hand, speaking words of comfort.

Just then, one of the spotters yelled, "Skua, ten o'clock!" Without missing a stroke, he switched his left hand to Mary's back, spun to the right, and got his binoculars up and on the approaching skua.

You can do only so much for somebody at the back rail, but you can still see birds!

A Walk in the Woods

There are always some anxieties when planning a bird-watching field trip. The date is set months in advance. You wonder if the weather will be decent that day. Will the birds show up? One mid-October morning, I led a group of twenty birdwatchers along the trails of the Joseph E. Wargo Nature Center. It's part of the Rice Creek Chain of Lakes Regional Park Reserve, located north of the Twin Cities in Lino Lakes.

Among the anxieties I've had in the past, the sight that greeted us at Wargo was a first: The parking lot was packed with police cars. We had to park along the entry road. Law enforcement people were being trained to search for an abducted child. Now I had another thing to worry about. Would the park be filled with police officers combing the woods? We'd be in each other's way, and any birds would probably be spooked. Staff at the Nature Center assured us that field exercises wouldn't start until noon. We'd be out of the woods by then.

We headed down the trail, a six-foot-wide swath of closely mowed grass. It was easy walking, but surprisingly spongy. It appeared that groundhogs and moles had burrowed under a good portion of the trail. We found the yellow crime scene tape designating search areas a little eerie. But there were birds. Dark-eyed juncos were everywhere. They're the dark grey birds with the white tummies and outer tail feathers that flash when they dart to cover.

Birdwatchers appreciate the opportunity to compare similar birds. We had a couple of chances to see such birds near each other, which is a good study for beginners and a refresher for others. The first comparative study involved a ruby-crowned and a golden-crowned kinglet in the same tree. Kinglets are tiny, three- to four-inch birds that flit around constantly, feeding on small insects and spiders. Seeing both together during their fall migration was a real treat. The ruby-crowned kinglet has a white eye-ring, which gives it a "big-eyed" look. The golden-crowned has a dark line extending through its eye and a whitish eyebrow stripe above it. It's really helpful if you can get a good look at the head. This was a very good chance for our group to study the differences.

Our next study involved three birds: a white-breasted nuthatch, a red-breasted nuthatch, and a brown creeper. These birds crawl on tree trunks and larger branches, searching for insects and larvae. The white-breasted nuthatch seems far more common, and is larger, plump with a dark cap, blue-gray back and white belly. It's a frequent visitor to feeders and has a nasal "yank" call.

By contrast, the red-breasted nuthatch favors conifers. It's smaller with a dark eye stripe, a prominent white eyebrow, and a rusty reddish belly. The call is more nasal than the white-breasted nuthatch. Although nuthatches can maneuver up or down a tree trunk, the sparrow-sized and sparrow-colored brown creeper can only climb up. The creeper has stiff tail feathers that help it along in its ascent. It's a very shy bird with a faint, high pitched "seee" call. You'll notice the brown creeper most often as it flies to the base of a tree to begin its upward climb.

As our group hiked, we also noticed a lot of upright dead trees. That's great habitat for woodpeckers, although the only species everyone in the group saw was the downy woodpecker. Just a few folks saw its larger relative, the hairy woodpecker. So we didn't get a good side-by-side study of these two. I scanned the woods for the signs of motion that would reveal the presence of birds.

I saw a black and white, crow-sized bird swoop through the trees. "Pileated woodpecker!" I shouted, but I didn't call out in time for anyone else to see it. Could it have been a vagrant ivory-billed blown north by one of the Gulf hurricanes? In my dreams.

A few feet farther along the trail, we walked into the premier viewing event of the morning. I noticed a robin-sized bird hopping through some brush just off the trail. We watched as it dodged in and out of the thicket. Suddenly it hopped out onto a perch at about eye level with a tree trunk behind it, about fifteen feet from the trail.

The hermit thrush posed for all to view. Brown overall, with heavy spotting on the breast, it raised its rufous tail and then slowly lowered it. That tail lifting and lowering is one of the identifying traits of the hermit thrush.

After watching it for a couple of minutes and studying its face, someone in the group spoke quietly to the bird and asked, "Now can we see the left side?" The bird obliged by turning its head to the right so we could get the left profile. Amazing. As it flew off, we saw another join it, so there had been two of them. "Must not have been a real hermit," I remarked.

We had a beautiful day, good companionship, and several opportunities for comparative study of similar birds capped by a private seminar conducted by a very willing, cooperative, and handsome migrating hermit thrush. The police training exercise was successful, but their evidence had been planted.

Birdwatchers, on the other hand, have no guarantees, no one "planting" birds. We depend on the birds themselves to show up, and, indeed, they did. The officers found what they were looking for, and so did we. A very successful day all around.

Trails and Trials

"*If we're not back* in an hour, send out the dogs," I laughed. "The ones with the brandy casks around their necks!" Well, we weren't back in an hour, and they didn't send any dogs.

Jean and I had been driving home from Lake Superior's North Shore after a late summer respite. As we entered Duluth, she asked if we were going to visit Hawk Ridge. Great idea! So we headed up to Skyline Parkway.

The folks at the Hawk Ridge overlook hadn't seen many hawks that morning, but they'd spotted an osprey, six sharp-shinned hawks, and an eagle. "Come on, Jean," I said, "I'll take you up to the summit. You can see the whole valley from up there."

"How long a hike is it?" she asked.

"Not bad," I said. "There're some high rock steps to climb, but I think you can negotiate them." That's when I made my remark about sending out the dogs. We headed down the road to the trailhead for an impromptu walk in the woods. Impromptu, yes, and, as it turned out, not too smart. It began to sprinkle.

"Maybe we shouldn't go if it's going to rain," Jean said.

"I don't think this is going to last. We can always turn back," I reasoned. (We'd left our rain gear in the car.) "Here's the Blue Trail. This is the trail we want. See the blue dot on the trees? That's how they mark the trails."

The drizzle stopped. The trail wound gradually uphill, with an occasional rock buried in the pathway, like an easy portage in the

Boundary Waters. Soon we crossed a trail with red dots on the trees. "I think the Red Trail goes directly to the summit, but the Blue Trail is more gradual, less rock climbing."

We hiked for quite a while. Jean saw the south end of a north-bound raccoon. I saw a northern flicker, showing me the white blaze on its rump as it darted away. The path rose gently, and then began to head downhill. "We're not going to get to the summit by going downhill, are we?" Jean asked.

"You're probably right," I said, "but maybe it winds around below the summit and then heads uphill again." (I hadn't brought a map.)

We came to a clearing with blue dots and big blue arrows on power poles showing where the Blue Trail crossed it. The clearing went up-hill under the power lines, but I wasn't sure it was really a trail, or in what direction it was going. (I'd left the compass in the car.)

I led us along the Blue Trail, hoping to find another trail, some way back to the main road without turning around and retracing our steps. Must be a guy thing. All at once we came upon the end of the trail: a bare, steep slope. Cautiously, I headed down first, legs spread and my arms out. I told Jean to lean against my back to slow herself. Suddenly, I heard her feet go out from under her, and down she went. She said she was okay. (Our first aid kit was in the car.) Helping her to her feet, we negotiated the rest of the embankment together.

The trail then joined what looked like an old logging road. I turned, arbitrarily, to the right. (Again, no compass and no map.) There was evidence that this wider trail had been used by horseback riders. We tried not to step in the evidence.

We were gradually going downhill, so I figured we'd eventually meet the Skyline Parkway. Clearly, we weren't getting to the sum-mit today. Then we heard voices. Maybe horses and riders? A couple of guys on mountain bikes came barreling down the trail. We asked whether this trail would get us to the parkway and back up to the overlook.

"Yes, but you'll be at the bottom of the parkway. It's about a fif-teen minute walk." At this point, that sounded okay. Looking back, their estimate was very low. But at least now we were heading in the right direction. The horse trail followed a winding creek that spilled through rocky canyons. It was a lovely walk, but long. (I'd left my camera in the car, too.) We could have used an energy bar or a drink of water. (By now you've figured out where that stuff was, right?)

We reached the parkway and headed uphill again. A marker read "3 Miles." I'd seen a start line near the overlook, so I guessed we still had three miles to go. Naturally, it started to rain again. Soon we passed the start of the White Trail. "That's the trail we should have taken!" I exclaimed excitedly. "There it is!"

"Do you want to take it now?" Jean asked, breathing hard from the uphill climb, but trying to show some limited enthusiasm.

"No."

"Good."

A mile or so farther, we came upon the Yellow Trail. "No, *this* is the trail we should have taken! See, the signpost says 'Ridge Loop Trail.' That's it!"

This was the third time I'd found the "right" trail. Jean was just glad we weren't going to try it. We'd already hiked plenty. The drizzle slowed. When we finally arrived at the overlook, one of the staff was showing a sharp-shinned hawk to some people. She released it. It climbed high above the ridge, just a speck against the clouds.

We'd been gone over two and a half hours. The trail map at the overlook showed we'd basically made a wide loop around the summit. Had we taken the Red Trail to the right when we crossed it, we would have intersected the Yellow Trail, the Ridge Loop Trail.

As our good friend and neighbor Jim always asks, "What have we learned today?" Well, we learned that an impulsive trip into the woods could have gone wrong. "Impromptu" had turned into a whole lot of wandering. When you're birding or out for a hike in a new area, be prepared. Look for a map or ask someone. Bring water, a compass, snacks, and perhaps a whistle. Bring a first aid kit if there is rugged terrain ahead. And rain gear, if appropriate. Camera is optional.

Next time we plan to take a few minutes to go back to the car for the essentials.

Purple Sandpiper Road Trip

Winter birding is a bit of a challenge. So what could compel three Minnesotans to drive four hundred miles to Waukegan, Illinois, in sub-freezing January temperatures? That was the question my pals and I were asked just after sunrise on a frigid Monday in January 2007. The answer, of course, was a chance to see a rare bird.

Staff at the Waukegan Port District found Bill, Jeff, and me standing on one of the docks which jut into the cold, dark waters of Lake Michigan: Three guys with three spotting scopes aimed toward the rocky shoreline.

"What are you looking at?" an employee asked.

"There's a purple sandpiper working the shoreline. It's a very rare bird," we told him. In fact, in our collective sixty years of birdwatching, none of us had ever seen one. It was feeding among a flotilla of mallards, carefully avoiding nips from a few of the females.

The purple sandpiper spends its summers on the shores of Greenland. In the winter, it appears along the east coast of the United States and sporadically along the shorelines of the Great Lakes. An otherwise dumpy, dark bird, the purple shows in the brief breeding season, and then only in good light. It's smaller than a robin, but just as pudgy. The bill is long and sharp; the tail very short. This sandpiper forages for food right along the waterline around rocks, jetties, and breakwaters, dodging the lapping waves. It picks off crustaceans and other tidbits clinging to the rocks. Because it's such a dark, non-descript bird, if it doesn't move it's very difficult to spot among the rocks and waves.

My buddies and I monitor a couple of rare bird hotlines, which is how we knew of several purple sandpiper sightings that winter along the western shore of Lake Michigan. The most recent sighting had been in Waukegan's port area, just north of Chicago. So, late on Saturday night, the three of us held a conference call. Jeff was pretty excited about finding the bird and, if we missed it there, one had been reported in Indiana and another in Ohio.

"Heck," I joked, "we could keep going all the way to the East Coast where the sandpiper is more likely to show up." But I secretly hoped Jeff had been kidding about Indiana and Ohio.

We departed the Twin Cities about 5:30 a.m. on a Sunday and arrived at the Waukegan Port just after noon. We spent several hours scouring the shoreline, the riprap, the docksides, looking for any sign of movement or even just a gray-brown lump sitting there. No luck. We decided to head up to Racine, Wisconsin, to Wind Point, where a purple sandpiper had been reported earlier.

We met another birder there who said the sandpiper hadn't been seen for a few days. But he did know where we could find a laughing gull in the Racine harbor. That would be a life bird for Jeff, so we followed the fellow through Racine to the harbor. The gulls were gone, and darkness was descending.

Jeff was despondent. "It's over," he said. "No sandpiper, no laughing gull. What a bummer."

Bill asked how long we'd have to put up with Jeff's whining. Jeff was *my* buddy; Bill hadn't traveled with him before. It was good-natured teasing, and Jeff joined in, giving as good as he got.

After supper, Bill called home and asked his wife to check the Internet for any reports of the purple sandpiper in Wisconsin or Illinois. She found a notice that the sandpiper had been seen at the Waukegan Port ten minutes after we had left. It had flown in (from location unknown) and stayed working the shoreline for quite some time. Argh!

Then and there we had our plan for the next day. We reasoned that if the bird had come in late in the day, it would spend the night nearby and be up early ready to feed some more.

We resolved to be at the port at sunrise on Monday. And so we were. And so was the purple sandpiper. We watched the bird for several hours and then helped ourselves to the hospitality of the Port District offices to warm up and refill our coffee mugs.

Susan Petty, the receptionist, asked Bill how we had found out about the bird. Bill described how we monitor the birding hotline, learning that one had been sighted in Waukegan. "We decided to head out to see it," he said.

"Ah," she said. "Road trip!"

Exactly!

We revisited the Racine harbor as we headed back to Minnesota and there, as advertised, was the laughing gull. This was very likely the first winter sighting of a laughing gull in Wisconsin, another Atlantic coast bird. Jeff got his second life bird for the trip. The whining declined dramatically.

And we didn't have to go all the way to the East Coast to find these birds. They were right there on the Middle Coast, much closer to us Minnesotans and an option for the January doldrums of birdwatching.

Dawn of the Lesser Sandhill Cranes

Drew and I looked across the river. As far as the eye could see, we viewed what looked like huge clusters of shrubs on the sandbars. They all appeared to be the same size, rounded, and uniformly gray. But it was an hour before sunrise and gray was the dominant shade. A glance through our binoculars, however, told us these weren't shrubs. They were roosting cranes, each with its head tucked under its wing.

My son and I were in a blind on the banks of the Platte River near Kearney, Nebraska, one late March to witness the gathering of lesser sandhill cranes. More than a half million cranes migrate north from the Gulf Coast and Mexico. They stop over on the Platte to refuel and to strengthen or reestablish pair bonds before heading farther north to their nesting sites in northern Canada, northern Alaska, and even northern Siberia.

The lesser sandhill stands three and a half feet tall, gray with dark wingtips visible in flight. Its red crown is skin, not feathers, and its rear feathers puff out like a rooster's. We see the greater sandhill crane in Minnesota, five inches taller, with a longer bill. Last year's off-spring or colt migrates with its parents.

Family groups arrive in Nebraska at different times from mid-March to mid-April. Groups of sandhills spend about three weeks feeding on waste corn in the fields, seeds, and invertebrates, even mice. A lesser sandhill will add about twenty percent to its body weight during this time.

Those half million cranes use a ninety-mile stretch of the Platte River, a wide and shallow braided river that makes an ideal evening roost. Its wandering channels diverge and re-merge, creating sandbars all along its length. The cranes stand in the shallower water with deeper water around them, which serves as a barrier to predators and an early warning system if any dog, fox, or coyote splashes through while they sleep.

As dawn gradually brightened, we could see the cranes standing ankle deep in a slurry of fast-flowing ice chunks. Each balanced on one leg, looking like a gray flamingo. It was eighteen degrees in the blind, and we were very cold. I couldn't imagine trying to sleep upright on one foot in ice water all night.

According to our guide, the cranes chatter a bit all night long. As the sun rose higher, a few began to raise their heads and look around. Some were leaping and dancing, alone or in pairs. The males were trying to impress the ladies or were challenging other males for dominance. Maybe it was just to keep warm!

Cranes usually take off in family groups. We sensed imminent departure when a group would raise their heads, extend their necks, and stand very erect. Then at some unseen signal, that cluster of cranes would unfold their huge wings and flap, flap, flap into the morning wind.

We were treated to an unusual sight on our first morning in the blind. We estimated that there were about 30,000 cranes roosting in the section of the river we could see to the west.

Just as the sun cleared the horizon, wave after wave of flapping cranes lifted from the roosting masses, starting in the distance and rippling down river toward us. It was like sports fans doing the wave in a stadium except these "fans" didn't sit back down. They jumped into the air and just kept going, with their loud rattling calls echoing across the river. Soon we saw the explanation. An immature bald eagle came gliding low over the river. This strategy reveals any of the sick or wounded that can't get off the water, which may provide the eagle with an opportunity for a meal later in the day.

Evening viewing of the cranes was an entirely different experience.

Cranes came in from their distant feeding areas, miles off the river, to a few staging areas near the river. These bordering fields and wetlands provided them with a bedtime snack before heading for the Platte. The groups of cranes looked like streams of smoke against the fading sky. I estimated two thousand in one flock.

After the disk of the sun had dropped below the horizon, one family group finally decided it was time for bed and landed on a sandbar in the middle of the river. As more groups passed over, they saw that those below looked safe and sound, so they dropped in to join them. Soon the assembly had grown to a hundred birds or so, with more establishing new groups on other sandbars. Within an hour, most of the cranes were out of the sky and on the river. They shuffled about a little, walking out into the shallow water and settling in for the night.

The next morning, Drew and I headed back home and reviewed our experience. We both agreed that seeing and hearing thousands of cranes take to the air was awe-inspiring. For years I'd been asked if I'd been down to the Platte River to see the cranes in migration. When I'd answer no, I'd invariably be told, "You've got to go. It's a once-in-a-lifetime experience!" I decided I wasn't getting any younger. Drew was eager to go, so we made the trip.

It *was* a once in a lifetime experience to see 30,000 cranes all together in an ancient ritual. Truly inspirational. But it's also a ten-hour drive. I don't think I need do it again.

Midnight Sun on the Churchill River

We sat on the retaining wall on the south shore of the Churchill River, each sipping from his own bottle of Bailey's Irish Cream. We were celebrating my birthday, looking out across the river as small icebergs drifted up the river with the high tide in Hudson Bay.

On the far shore was Fort Prince of Wales. Beluga whales swam by from time to time, ghostly white, just below the swirling surface of the water. It was nearly midnight; the sky was still bright enough to see clearly. A canoe hove into view, coming down river and working toward the north bank. There were three people in it, all paddling. None wore a life jacket, but they did give the icebergs in the river wide berth, which showed some measure of caution. We had seen bergs suddenly tumble and roll without warning, creating a surge of waves around them.

My buddies, Bill and Joel, and I had travelled to Churchill, Manitoba, to see some unique birds, so belugas and crazy canoeists weren't high on our list. Many birds that migrate through Minnesota in the spring head up to the Churchill area to breed. Once there, the males come into their striking plumage and sing their territorial songs, trying to attract a mate. We heard the melodic song of the gray-cheeked thrush, a tune that harmonizes with itself as it tumbles down the scale and leaves you awestruck. They don't sing on migration, so we don't get to hear that song back in Minnesota.

Churchill, population 813 in 2011, is more famous as the polar bear capital of the world. Over 12,000 tourists come to see the polar bears each year. We, on the other hand, preferred not to see any. We were told that a bear had been in town the morning of the day we arrived, but had left before we got there. Any time we were along the shore of Hudson Bay, we carefully scanned the icebergs frozen into the water along the shore. Although it was difficult to judge the size of a berg across the monochromatic landscape, many had a rather hunched polar bear appearance and yellowish tint.

We watched each berg long enough to make sure it wasn't moving. It was wise to be alert. At the mouth of the Churchill River, where it empties into Hudson Bay, there were signs warning visitors of the possibility of polar bear encounters, along with an emergency phone reputedly connected directly to a rescue line. I wondered how long it would take rescuers to arrive and how much of me a bear would be able to eat in that time.

Hudson Bay is the world's second largest inland sea. Even though it's salty, the surface freezes over from mid-December till mid-June, halting maritime shipping for those months. It was the growth center for the ice sheet that covered northern North America during the last Ice Age.

Churchill has only about fifteen miles of paved roads, with another fifty miles of graded roads in the "greater Churchill" area. None of these roads connects with the outside world, so you can only get to Churchill by plane or rail, which is forty hours from Winnipeg. The town is situated on permafrost. Telephone poles are paired in an A-shaped configuration and sit on the surface, not driven into the soil. The train doesn't run until the tracks have settled down after the spring freeze-thaw cycle. The runway at the airport is crushed rock, making for quite a bumpy ride on landing.

The polar bear "jail," a couple of Quonset huts, is at the airport. Bears that wander into town, and can't be persuaded to wander back out are kept there until ice conditions are right to release them into the wild. It was another reminder that visitors needed to be cautious. Our rental vehicle was a thirteen-year old pickup truck with few miles on it. After all, where could it have gone? We used it to explore the spruce forests, tundra, and shoreline.

When we arrived in Churchill, it was having one of its warmest ever June days. The temperature was nearly 80°, but dropped to the more normal 30s the next day, along with wind and snow flurries. But there were very few black flies or mosquitos. That's really an important consideration when planning a trip to Churchill. Apparently from late June on, the insects can be overwhelming and mosquito netting and long sleeves are *de rigueur.*

The first life birds we saw were Arctic terns, lots of them swooping over us as we stood on the shore of a pond on the outskirts of town. Over four days, I saw more than a dozen life birds, including Arctic loon, common eider, black scoter, spruce grouse, ruddy turnstone, red-necked phalarope, Smith's longspur, two different jaegers (both parasitic and long-tailed), and four gull species (little gull, Thayer's gull, Iceland gull, and Ross's gull).

Sighting the Ross's was very special. It was my 300th life bird, and a beauty at that. We found one resting on a snow field in the shadow of some spruces, visible from the highway. Churchill is one of the few places where a Ross's gull may show up in the summer. It's a small, delicate gull with a thin, dark collar that rings its head and neck, and has a rosy pink wash on the chest and underside. It was one of the target birds that inspired our trip in the first place.

With the very short growing season in the boreal forest (or taiga biome, as it's also known), a ten-foot tall tree may a hundred years old. Trees seldom reach a height of twenty feet. Curiously, a rather large shorebird named the Hudsonian godwit seemed to favor a perch on the top of a stunted spruce tree. Seeing a plump shorebird gingerly balanced atop an ancient, slender black spruce was always a surprise. The Hudsonian godwit is about sixteen inches long and weighs eleven ounces, with a bill about a fourth of its body length. It's about the size and weight of a pileated woodpecker.

By the end of our stay, we suffered a problem common in Arctic regions. The long daylight hours inspired us to just keep going while we could still see. But about 2 p.m. on the last day, we had to head back to the Polar Motel to crash for a couple hours.

At breakfast the next morning, three local Aboriginal women in the restaurant kept eyeing us and chattering with each other. Finally one of them told the other two she wanted the big one (that would be Joel, a very large man). Bill and I snorted. Joel allowed how it might be time to head for the airport.

"Surveys, Research, and Rescue"

Searching for Golden Eagles

One snowy Saturday in January, I searched for golden eagles along the Mississippi River with two women and a dog. The women were my birding buddy, Val, and our mutual friend, Kim. The dog was Finnegan, or Finn for short. Finn came with Kim.

Kim claims Finn is a mixed breed of wolf and Jack Russell terrier. It must have been a delicate "mixing," with emphasis on the Jack Russell genes because Finn was kind of short, reddish, and very alert. Whenever we peered out the car windows looking for eagles, Finn was excited to see what everyone was looking at.

He turned out to be an excellent wild turkey alarm. The first flock we found was crossing the road ahead of us, some dropping out of the trees. There must have been thirty of them. Finn really wanted to chase them and barked like crazy to let them know he would be hot on their trail if he could just get out of the car.

We didn't see any golden eagles that day, but not for lack of trying. We were participating in the annual golden eagle survey sponsored by the National Eagle Center in Wabasha, Minnesota. More than a hundred observers were out surveying specific territories in southeastern Minnesota and western Wisconsin. We found out later that other volunteers spotted seventy golden eagles!

As the national symbol, bald eagles get all the attention, but golden eagles are just as exciting to see, and less common. They're about the same size, too. But a bald eagle's head and neck extend beyond its body more than half the length of its tail in flight, whereas the golden eagle's head and neck extend less than half the tail length. Golden eagles have a uniformly dark brown body and wings. Young birds may have white patches on the underside of the wings near the ends, and may have a white band at the base of the tail, as well. Both mature and juveniles have a golden sheen on the head and nape of the neck.

Golden eagles breed from the Rockies west all the way to northern Alaska, including the far north of eastern Canada. They migrate short to mid-range distances in the fall. Most of the western birds come south along the Rockies. Some roam as far as the mid-Dakotas. Eastern golden eagles winter very locally in the eastern United States, but Minnesota and Wisconsin haven't been high on the list of known wintering sites. Hence, one reason for the survey.

Our territory was Pierce County, Wisconsin, right across the Mississippi River from Red Wing, Minnesota. Because this territory hadn't been surveyed before, we used topographic maps to find likely winter habitat. We cruised more than a hundred miles of back roads and valleys. Many of the streams in the county feeding into the Mississippi River have formed coulees, steep-sided valleys with loose rocks at the base of the slopes.

Golden eagles don't fish like bald eagles; they prefer terrestrial prey. They hunt on the south and west-facing slopes of the coulees, on what are called "goat prairies." These areas have thin soil over the bedrock, which can support grasses and small shrubs, but very few trees. The winter sun warms the hillsides, drawing prey to these goat prairies. Perfect hunting ground for wintering golden eagles.

At a training session at the Eagle Center a week before the survey, Scott Mehus, Education Program Specialist, quizzed us on what we thought were the main food sources for the golden eagle. We readily, and correctly, guessed rabbits and squirrels. But we were stumped on the next most frequent prey species until someone meekly offered wild turkey.

"What?" he asked, with a surprised look on his face. "You think a golden eagle weighing eight to ten pounds could take down a turkey which might weigh as much as fifteen pounds? Are you kidding me? Well, you happen to be absolutely . . . right!"

He said that when he sees a flock of turkeys, he can judge if a golden eagle is in the area by watching how the turkeys act. If they hang close to the woods or run for cover, look up for a golden eagle. If they're just foraging in the middle of a clearing, you can be pretty sure there's no golden around.

Interestingly, turkeys seem to know the difference between a golden and a bald eagle. The latter won't bother them. They ignore one if it flies over. Golden eagles often perch in the trees on the northern or eastern side of a bluff. This allows them to use the terrain as a screen to conceal their approach as they swing up over the crest right above the goat prairie on the sunny side of the hill. It's a sneak attack.

If you find yourself in southeastern Minnesota in winter, look for turkeys on the side of a bluff on a goat prairie. If you see them begin to run for the woods, there may be a golden eagle overhead.

Chimney Swift Sit

I participated in a lot of bird surveys one summer. I hiked the same route once a week for two months, bushwhacked across prairies, participated in bird counts that started at dawn, and joined owl counts that began after dark.

Finally, I had a more relaxing survey: Minnesota's first Chimney Swift Sit. I only had to find a likely chimney, pull up a lawn chair at dusk, and watch for swifts ducking in to roost for the night. They're easy to spot with their black swept-back wings and flying cigar-like appearance in the air. Their chittering call matches their nervous flittering flight.

Audubon Minnesota began its Chimney Swift Conservation Project in 2009 with the goal of educating folks with chimneys that swifts might use and teaching others who were interested how to build a roost site for swifts. Part of this project was the Chimney Swift Sit with specific dates when volunteers would count the number of swifts using a roosting site. There were three nights each in August and September.

The first evening, my friend Bonnie and I scouted some likely chimneys, including the James J. Hill house on Summit Avenue in St. Paul, one among several huge mansions along Summit with lots of tall chimneys, many of which don't have screens over the top. They looked like tempting roosting sites. We saw and heard swifts overhead, but none made a move toward any of the chimneys. Then we tried an apartment building on Selby Avenue whose chimney was used by some thirty swifts last year. Again, there were swifts in the air zooming past in small groups, but none took a dive into the chimney.

We learned that we could probably scout out only one location per night. By the time we figured out that none of the passing swifts were going to drop in, it was too dark to get to another location in time to see roosting activity.

The next night I went alone to a church in Lauderdale. It had a relatively short chimney, but it looked like it had a large opening. I saw several swifts pass overhead, but none went down the chimney. Then a group of about twenty swifts assembled and headed south down the street, so I made a mental note to check chimney sites farther south later in the week.

On the third and last night, four of us drove down to the Villa Maria Retreat and Conference Center to count all the swifts we knew from experience used its chimney as a roost site. One in our group, Paul, had been there a few weeks earlier and had counted more than a hundred, even though he arrived after they'd already started going in. We didn't hit that number. Bonnie saw one go in and two come out, so her count was minus one. I figured I'd seen three to five go in. What happened?

Our guess was that since it was a very overcast night with drizzle on and off, the birds had gone to bed early and the ones we saw were a couple of wild and crazy teenagers staying out as late as they could. There may have been more, but as it gets darker, it gets harder to see the swifts. Paul says it's like an eye test, continuously focusing on the middle distance above the chimney with the hope of spotting the quick drop of a dark bird against a darkening sky. Did I just see what I thought I saw?

One evening after the Villa outing, Jean and I decided to walk Buffy down the Eustis Street hill to look for any action around the Newmech Company's chimney. I'd never seen any swifts there before, but I suspected that the flock of twenty from earlier in the week might have been heading there.

We saw a few swifts fly over at twenty-five minutes before sunset.

The largest group was six or eight heading farther south down Eustis. Then at nine minutes after sunset, one swift dropped down the chimney. Fist pump! In the next eighteen minutes, five more swifts dropped in, two flew back out, and so we had a net roosting population of four. I was elated. This site had been a bit of a scientific guess on my part.

If you ever take part in such a count, it's important to do some scouting before the actual count period. If a site is on private property, let the owners know what you're up to. While this survey is called a Chimney Swift Sit, I didn't bring a chair or box to sit on, which wasn't too swift on my part. It was wearying to stand around in one place for an hour waiting for those flying cigars.

Get out there and pick a likely chimney, bring a chair. I hope you'll be in double or triple digits in your own Chimney Swift Sit survey.

Christmas Bird Count

We started well before dawn in a local woods, hooting and calling (and watching yard lights go on in the neighborhood as folks wondered what all the hooting was about). You might wonder as well.

It was just my team on the annual Christmas Bird Count, trying to get an owl to respond so we could add it to our count for the day. After hiking the woods at dawn, we retired to a Perkin's restaurant for breakfast to warm up and plan the rest of our day till sunset. We were responsible for identifying and counting all the birds in our part of the fifteen mile circle assigned to the St. Paul (North) CBC.

I enjoy several things about participating in the annual CBC. I get to meet new people and introduce beginning birders to the hobby. I remember one young man looking above the car as he stepped out and asking about the bird in the tree over us. It was his first sighting of a sharp-shinned hawk! We were all pretty psyched. The CBC also gives me a chance to explore parts of the northern Twin Cities metro I normally don't visit.

It seems that every year's count is different, depending on the weather. We've had years when it was so cold we couldn't keep the side windows of the car from frosting up. We'd roll them down a half-inch and try to peek out the gap to see and count birds as we drove from one site to the next. Some years there are so few birds that we end up counting wooden woodpeckers nailed to trees, brass eagles above garage doors and on flagpoles, and pink flamingoes left standing in the yard. Hey, a bird is a bird! We're born to count! (Of course, these counts are just for our amusement and to boost our morale.)

We like to encourage winter bird feeding. One year we tried distributing coupons for a free five-pound bag of birdseed at the doorstep of any house sporting an empty bird feeder. It was awkward marching up and sticking the coupon in the front door after sitting at the curb training five sets of binoculars on the yard. We only handed out two coupons and haven't repeated the practice since.

Taking part in the annual CBC is an opportunity to participate in one of the longest running citizen science projects. Toward the end of the 19th century, many folks spent the week between Christmas and New Year's shooting everything in sight on something called a "side hunt." I've seen photos of piles of birds and mammals blasted into oblivion all in the name of "family fun."

This didn't sit well with ornithologist Frank Chapman. He proposed that instead of shooting everything that flew over, why not count them and see who gets the highest count? It started in 1900 with twenty-seven counters holding twenty-five counts in sites from Toronto, Canada, to Pacific Grove, California. Among them, they totaled ninety species.

That tradition of counting, not shooting, grew and spread. As of 2010, there were nearly 60,000 observers in more than 2,100 CBC locations in the western hemisphere, identifying 665 species one year in the United States alone. Data from CBCs have highlighted dramatic drops in the populations of many birds, including meadowlarks, boreal chickadees, and evening grosbeaks.

Some years ago, the drop in peregrine falcon counts led researchers to discover that DDT caused thin eggshells for raptors. This led to a ban on the insecticide in 1972 and the eventual recovery of the peregrine, even here in Minnesota.

The CBC is always scheduled between December 14th and January 5th. The coordinator assigns you to a team, making an effort to mix beginners with more experienced birders, so new folks can feel they'll be able to have fun and contribute. Val Cunningham, birdwatcher, field trip leader, and writer from Como Park in St. Paul has been participating in the St. Paul Audubon CBC for more than twenty years.

"I love doing it," she says. "Even though when it's over I ask myself, 'Why?' But I forget about the cold by March, and I'm ready for the next one. It's a major National Audubon Society effort. I feel like I'm giving something back to birds with this citizen science survey. And it's a great break in all the holiday craziness."

If you're homebound or don't have time to tour the city, you can participate as a feeder watcher. And there's usually a potluck supper at the end of the day, where people swap sightings, tally counts, and tell the occasional fib, like "It was a roseate spoonbill. I'm sure of it."

Find a Christmas Bird Count and join one of the longest running citizen science projects. Prepare to be surprised at how many birds are out and about.

As Val says, "It's fun to see what birds are doing on a winter's day."

Counting Cranes

It was still dark at 5:20 in the morning. A light rain had stopped ten minutes earlier. There were no other cars on the road, so I pulled across the oncoming lane and parked on the left shoulder. My assignment was to spend the next two hours looking and listening for sandhill cranes.

The sandhill makes a striking impression both on land and in the air. This mostly gray bird with white cheeks stands four feet tall. Its fluff of tail feathers looks like a bustle. What resembles a red cap on its head is actually a bald spot (no wonder I like them). The sandhill usually has a rusty color on its body, called "staining," caused when the bird preens itself with a muddy beak. They often feed in swamps and wetlands that have iron compounds in the mud, thus the reddish-brown stains.

In flight, sandhill cranes stretch out their necks and let their legs trail behind. They don't flap their wings in a steady down and up rhythm. The upstroke is much faster than the downstroke. This is one of the best ways to separate a sandhill crane in flight from a great blue heron. The heron displays more of a steady up and down pattern. The great blue also usually flies with its neck pulled back in an "S" crook, not stretched out like the crane.

The Midwest Crane Count began in 1976, sponsored by the International Crane Foundation (ICF) in Baraboo, Wisconsin. All the counters throughout the Midwest go out on the same Saturday morning in April and count from 5:30 to 7:30 a.m. Any cranes seen or heard during that time period are reported back to the ICF. In addition to sandhill cranes, counters keep watch for evidence of whooping cranes, which are a bit taller than sandhills and all white with black wing tips and a red face. Counters are given very specific requirements for documenting any whooping crane sightings. The whooping crane is rare and is just coming back from near extinction. My assigned territory was Poplar Lake County Park, an undeveloped park on the northern edge of St. Paul's Ramsey County.

I did a preliminary survey of the area the week before the count and didn't see any trails, but I hiked in for a ways on the east side until I had a good view of the lake itself. Last year's grasses had been swept down by winter winds and snows, hiding uneven ground and hummocks surrounded by water puddles. Although it wasn't an easy trek, I figured I'd be able to negotiate it on "count Saturday," even in the dark before dawn.

But I didn't anticipate the rain. Before I left home on Saturday, I'd packed my rain pants. Even so, I wasn't eager to hike through the wet grass. I decided to listen at first from the road at the eastern edge of the park. If I heard or saw cranes, maybe I wouldn't have to hike at all.

After parking on the left shoulder, I refilled my coffee cup, got my clipboard ready, and, with binoculars in hand, stepped into the pre-dawn darkness. I could hear a woodcock calling with a "peent-peent" that reminded me of nighthawks in the summer. I also heard song sparrows, pheasants, and turkeys.

Then at 5:35 a.m., right after my count period officially began, I heard them: Sandhill cranes doing their croaky call in the distance, probably on the other side of Poplar Lake. I was ecstatic! The rumored presence of sandhill cranes in the park had been confirmed. I noted the time and type of call they made on my official ICF Crane Count Data Sheet. I didn't have to hike at all.

Cranes typically make three kinds of calls. First is the contact call. The adults are just keeping in touch with one another or reassuring new fledglings that all is well. The second is the guard call, used to warn away a predator or drive another crane out of a couple's nest area. The third, a duet between two cranes, is the unison call, which strengthens a pair bond in preparation for mating and nesting. I was pretty sure I was hearing the unison call, indication of a nesting pair in the area. The calls repeated every fifteen minutes or so for the entire two-hour count period. I posted the information on the Minnesota Ornithologists' Union website that afternoon.

I returned on Sunday morning to the same roadside location with son Drew to see if he could hear the cranes, too. We got there a little after six o'clock. A few minutes after our arrival, a white car pulled in behind ours. Out stepped Bob Janssen, Mr. Birding Minnesota, one of the most respected birdwatchers in the state.

I greeted him and introduced Drew. As I gave him my name, he said he knew me. He'd seen my Saturday posting on the MOU website and was surprised to see me back for a second day. Wow! Bob Janssen knew my name. My ego began to swell.

We all listened to birds, and then we heard the cranes call in the distance. I told Bob I had reported that as the unison call. He said that indeed it was. Another boost to my ego. I pointed out woodcock and snipe calls to my son, and Bob confirmed those as well. Then I told Drew I had heard another snipe call.

"No," Bob said, "I think that's a toad calling." Then he cupped his hands behind his ears, turned toward the sound, and repeated, "Yup, that's a toad calling."

A toad? I knew that frogs called, but *toads*? And they sound like snipe? Sudden ego deflation and yet another complication to listening to birdcalls. Not only would I have to screen out the chatter of chipmunks and red squirrels, I'd have to think about toad calls, too.

But I had to admit it was great to hear cranes a second day in a row, to have Drew hear them, and to have a great birder like Bob Janssen confirm my report of a unison call between a bonded pair of sandhill cranes. Next, how to filter out those dang toads?

Breeding Bird Survey

Drew and I had to be at the starting point at 4:58 a.m., no later. And that starting point was sixty miles west of the Twin Cities, just north of Cokato. If it rained or if the wind was too strong, we couldn't make the "run" that morning. We'd have to try another day, again no later than 4:58 a.m.

The strict rules were part of an annual Breeding Bird Survey (BBS) that we participated in along what is called the Knapp route, which covers twenty-five miles in Meeker and Wright counties. Part of the route passes through the city of Litchfield.

A Breeding Bird Survey covers the same route year after year, on a day between late May and early July, to gather data on what birds are using that territory for breeding sites. There are eighty-six routes in Minnesota, overseen by the U.S. Geological Survey (USGS) Patuxent Wildlife Research Center in Laurel, Maryland. The survey started in 1967.

Drew and I traveled by car, stopping every half mile, for a total of fifty stops. At each stop, we stepped out and looked and listened for three minutes, recording every bird we saw or heard.

When Drew and I first began doing the Knapp route several years ago, we left the Twin Cities about 3:00 in the morning so we'd be out at our starting point before that 4:58 a.m. official start time. The first year we ran into torrential rains just as we headed north out of Cokato. There would be no bird surveying that morning. We turned around, headed back home, and stopped at a pancake place for breakfast. We repeated the quest the next week, and the weather allowed us to run the route. After the first year, we learned to get a good night's sleep the night before in a nearby motel.

Each of the fifty stops is described in a one-line statement, passed down from the first person who made the survey. Some of those descriptions can get rather "folksy." For example, stop #5 is described as "Farm on right. Fire #16242. White flag pole right; phone pole left." The farm should be there from year to year. The fire number might change. But who can promise that the flagpole and phone pole will be there next year? Drew wisely brought along his GPS unit that first year and added the latitude and longitude for each of the stops. That helped us greatly in subsequent years.

I find it very interesting to see what changes in bird population have occurred from year to year. The route has become familiar to us, and we anticipate seeing certain species at the same points on the route. Sometimes we're surprised by a totally unexpected bird, such as the horned larks Drew discovered toward the end of our route the second year. The horned lark reminds me of a skinny meadowlark, brown and yellow. And it actually does have little feathery horns on each side of its head. They fly low, scurrying through plowed fields, and when they stop they're practically invisible. Drew's spotting them was quite a feat. Their song is a high-pitched tinkling sound.

We always hear more birds than we see. But one of the more bizarre sounds we encountered was at a stop where we heard a loud, screaming "Yeow!" What the heck? We looked around. The call repeated several times. Then we saw them. Walking along the fence line were two peacocks! Yard birds! We've seen white pelicans on a small lake along the BBS route and usually spot some in flight over the town of Howard Lake on our way back home from our territory.

The USGS gives us a bright orange window card for the car to help explain to passersby and residents who we are and why we're stopping along their roads. I imagine it's a little unnerving to see a car parked at the end of your driveway and two guys standing there with binoculars at 5:30 in the morning.

I enjoy participating in citizen-scientist projects like the BBS.

It gives me a chance to apply my hobby of birdwatching to further a broader understanding of our environment by identifying trends in bird populations and by documenting the effects of habitat changes. For example, trend data for Minnesota (1980–2006) on the USGS website shows that redheaded woodpeckers, gray partridges, and yellow-headed blackbirds are in decline, while house finches, American white pelicans, and red-bellied woodpeckers are increasing in number.

Participating in projects like this one is a lot of fun. It's a terrific way to meet people and find out more about birds, all the while helping scientists better understand the status of bird populations and their distribution.

Bird Banding 101

Next time you have two nickels in your pocket or purse, take them in the palm of your hand and feel their "heft." What you have there is the weight of the average male house wren, that small brown bird with a great singing voice. Two nickels weigh ten grams.

Add a dime to your hand and you've actually exceeded the weight of a lady house wren, which averages twelve grams. Jean had the chance to hold such a little wonder. We went to see how bird banding is done, and Jean was allowed to release the wren after it was processed.

Ron Refsnider is part of a bird banding team at the Carl and Janet Schuneman Wildlife Area in Washington County, Minnesota. He's one of three thousand licensed master bird banders in the United States. He's also a U.S. Fish and Wildlife Service staffer, specializing in endangered species, including the gray wolf.

Birds are captured in mist nets twelve meters long by three meters high, which are designed to hang with loose pockets across the length. Refsnider's crew of eleven volunteers had sixteen nets set up throughout the wildlife area the morning Jean and I went there to watch.

When a bird flew into a net, it dropped into the pocket. The banding team then gently untangled the bird, put it into a small cloth sack that looked like a miniature pillowcase, and tied the top shut. The "bagged" birds were brought to the picnic shelter banding station, where Refsnider had set up his equipment and logbooks. A volunteer carefully removed the bird from the cloth bag and transferred it to a zippered mesh bag before weighing it.

Based on the species, Refsnider selected the appropriate leg band from a set of twenty-two different band sizes. He read the number embossed on the band so the volunteer could enter that number on the log sheet. After the weigh-in, he took the bird and, using special pliers, spread the selected band open. He then put it around the bird's leg and gently closed the band without putting pressure on the leg itself. While he had the bird in hand, he examined it and measured wing and tail length, dictating the information to the volunteer maintaining the log. Wing length alone is useful in determining the sex in some species.

He also held the bird belly up and gently puffed to raise the feathers on the bird's underside. This allowed him to examine several things. First was the amount of fat stored on the chest, which can give a clue to the bird's migratory status. If a bird retains a great deal of fat, it probably hasn't completed migration and will be taking off for points north as soon as it gets an evening with a favorable wind.

A bird with little or no fat reserve has either completed its migration or just arrived the previous evening. It will take a day or two off to replenish its fat stores before continuing on migration. Examining the chest also shows whether there is a "brood patch," a patch of skin where the blood supply lies very close to the surface. This indicates a female bird which has been sitting on eggs, warming them with her chest.

An examination just below the belly can reveal the sex of the bird. Males have what is called a cloacal protuberance, evident only during breeding season. Refsnider also looked at feather wear and color. Older, unmolted feathers are faded and lighter than newly replaced, relatively fresh feathers, another clue to the bird's age. The volunteer seated next to Refsnider entered all of these facts and statistics next to the band number on the log page. When all the measurements and assessments were completed, Refsnider either released the bird himself or handed it to another person to release.

To release a bird, it is turned right side up in one hand, with the other hand gently over the top as the handler steps away from the banding table into a clear area. When the upper hand is removed, the bird flies away, usually to a nearby tree where it spends a few moments realigning its feathers before heading off to continue its day. The entire process from weighing to release usually takes five to ten minutes. The house wren that Jean released had been banded the year before and had been caught twice already that morning. Refsnider supposed that the wren was feeding nestlings and the mist net was right on its route between nest and food source.

Refsnider bands birds year round at Elm Creek Park Reserve in western Hennepin County, Springbrook Nature Center in Fridley, and in his back yard. He's at Schuneman Marsh twice a year or so. All of Refsnider's bird banding is done on a volunteer basis. Refsnider is very interested in winter bird banding because it can reveal details about site fidelity; that is, how often birds return to the same sites in the winter. But he can't use mist nets in winter and has to resort to live traps near feeders or other food sources.

Banding birds is useful in research and management projects. It helps scientists study migration patterns, habitat preferences, breeding sites, behavior, social structure, disease and toxicology, lifespan, survival rate, reproduction success, and population growth. The federal government uses banding data collected from waterfowl to help determine hunting limits for different species. The first bird bander in America is generally agreed to be John James Audubon who, in 1883, tied silver cords around the legs of eastern phoebe nestlings in Philadelphia to see if they'd return to the same place next year. Several of them did.

Perhaps the next time you have a few coins in your hand, you'll think about how delicate those little birds around us really are. And if you happen to see a phoebe with a silver cord around its leg . . .

Birds In Flight

Pop quiz for birders: What's an alula? It sounds like a Hawaiian dance, or that pink thing that hangs down at the back of your throat, or a kid saying, "Alleluia." It's spelled the same backwards and forwards and is pronounced al-YOU-la. Think of a bird's wing as similar to an arm with the "finger" bones fused out at the end. The alula is at the "thumb." A small thumb-like bone called the pollex holds the alula feathers.

The alula is very important for steering and slowing down. It diverts the air stream over the wing surface to increase lift, especially when braking for a landing. Airplanes imitate nature with a slat, a small wing-shaped airfoil along the leading edge of each wing that's extended to increase lift during landing. It opens up a path for air to flow over the wing even though the plane is nosing up.

I'd never heard of the alula before, but I learned about it and a lot of other fascinating aspects of bird flight during a talk by wildlife biologist and photographer Carrol Henderson, the author of *Birds in Flight: The Art and Science of How Birds Fly*. Henderson has a collection of more than 70,000 photos of more than a thousand species of birds. In reviewing those photos, he found that he had hundreds that captured different aspects of birds in flight. He explained that high-speed photography has greatly enhanced our understanding of what happens when birds fly.

Henderson presented slides as he spoke about his research and talked about his book. One slide showed Canada geese surfboarding in for a landing with their alulas lifted, letting them control the rate of descent to the water. Henderson's high-speed photography also allowed him to illustrate how the feathers at the wing tips function like a propeller, flexing and twisting to provide forward thrust with the down stroke of the wing. In addition, he showed how wing position is adjusted depending on what the bird is attempting to do. For example, when a bird wants to hover in place, the wings are more V-shaped with the wingtips doing the fluttering to stay in place. The area of the wing closest to the body provides most of the lift while the area beyond the alula provides most of the propulsion. When hovering, lift isn't needed as much.

His book provides an intriguing explanation for why birds fly in V-formations, too. One illustration showed the circular vortex that curls off the wings of the lead bird, resulting in an extended tube of air that has an upward spin. The birds that follow on either side of the leader can use this tube to add lift to their own flight, passing on additional lift to the next bird. I think the longer leg of the V may be due to the wind direction at their altitude, which aides or dampens out the vortex effect.

How do the wing designs of different birds allow them to specialize? The ratio between wing length and width (aspect ratio) allows pelicans to glide along wave tops with very little effort (long and narrow wings). Pheasants, however, have short and wide wings that allow them to "pop up" when flushed, providing greater maneuverability. They get by with shorter glides.

How about how much weight a set of wings can carry? That's wing loading. Barn swallows are a good example, evidenced by their effortless gliding after insects. Water birds have high wing loading. The common loon needs to face the wind, run along the water and flap its wings like crazy in order to get into the air.

Much of the book compares bird flight to airplane flight in straightforward, easy-to-understand language with clear illustrations. He covers flight in what he calls soft science: Bernoulli's effect, lift across the wing, and the angle of attack of the wing to the direction of flight, the kinds of things most of us learned in high school science and promptly forgot.

I was captivated by wing details during the presentation. Henderson covers this and much more in his beautifully constructed book: feathers and bones, the tail's function, take-offs, and landings. The photos are gorgeous. There's a very complete index and bibliography.

Any bird lover, citizen scientist, or nature lover on your gift list would love this book. You'll probably want one for yourself as well.

Hunting for Red-headed Woodpecker Nests

One June morning I went into the woods with a couple of women. At my age that's as close as I'll get to a racy story. Bonnie, Val, and I were conducting a red-headed woodpecker nest survey at the Cedar Creek Ecosystem Science Reserve, a University of Minnesota study area near East Bethel, Minnesota.

An intern, who'd been to the site to film red-headed woodpecker nestlings, had marked the nest areas with little black circles on a satellite image map. There were six such circles in our assigned section of the map. Our goal was to locate the specific nest trees, gather data about the tree and its surrounding habitat, and see if there were other nest sites nearby.

Cedar Creek is in the Anoka Sand Plain. The access roads and trails are all sand. Getting close to the marked areas wasn't too much of a challenge. Getting near a nest tree itself, however, was a different matter. Red-headed woodpeckers seem to prefer nesting in oak savannahs: groups of trees in the midst of shorter undergrowth, witch hazel bushes, willows, poison ivy, and the like. Navigating this undergrowth is where cross-country hiking gets interesting.

Adding to the challenge was fallen timber concealed beneath more than three feet of dense growth. We really had to watch where we walked. Often I would step over a large limb only to discover there was another just as large right where I wanted to plant my other foot. Bonnie called them ankle-breakers. Regular controlled burns had charred those branches and limbs, so I got charcoal streaks on my pants, too. All in all, I did a lot of stumbling around.

Red-headed woodpeckers are cavity nesters. They seem to favor half-dead oak trees or totally dead standing snags. The nest hole can be anywhere from eight to eighty feet up in a tree that usually has very short understory growth beneath it. This may be so the birds can see potential predators, or so they can exit the nest hole and drop down a good ways to gain speed before they have to level off and flap their wings.

From the entry road, we'd seen a red-headed woodpecker fly toward one of the survey spots on our map. We wanted to get close to where that little black circle was marked on the map, then wait and watch. After walking north about a quarter mile into our territory, Bonnie and I left the road and headed to the west, cross-country. Val had it easier. She just went farther up the road to another potential site. The site Bonnie and I headed toward was about five hundred feet away through waist-high brush. There was a lot of stumbling, as expected, and changing of direction around fallen trunks, but we eventually arrived in the area where we had seen the red-headed woodpecker fly in.

There were a number of potential nest trees in the clearing, so we watched and waited to see the bird return, hoping to see which tree it visited before it left again. Was the adult carrying food on the way in? Did it crawl into a nest hole or only stick its head in? If not, maybe it's another tree. Could we find a potential nest hole in any one of those trees?

In this case, we saw the red-headed woodpecker enter the stub end of a limb that had broken off high up in the tree. The stub had been excavated down in from the breakoff point at the tip. Whenever we saw evidence of an active nest site, I bushwhacked over to the base of the tree, took a GPS reading and called it out to Bonnie. I then tied a shiny purple ribbon around the tree trunk to enable easier spotting next time we were there. Bonnie recorded more data, including the tree species, tree status (living / some percent dead / totally dead snag), tree height, cavity height, the direction it faced, and description of the understory. Then she took a photo of the tree.

We labored back to the road and caught up with Val. She'd seen a red-headed woodpecker come in, but it was unclear which tree it was visiting. We all moved back to a side road where we could still see the group of trees. Soon, one came in to a nearby tree, looked around for a while, then headed right toward a specific tree in the cluster and disappeared into a nest hole just out of our line of sight. Another hit!

Then we went farther north, hiked west again along the edge of a meadow (avoiding the damp slogging through underbrush for a while), and eventually back south to another oak cluster in a clearing. Again, we saw an adult come in and enter a nest hole. We were really getting good at this!

Next we returned to the southern edge of our territory where three black circles awaited us. With a bit of patient watching (actually hearing the peeping of some nestlings waiting for mom or dad to return with breakfast), we successfully marked the remaining three nest trees, although we had run out of purple ribbon. We would have to rely on Bonnie's photos for reference.

Our score: Six for six! We were all quite pleased. We looked forward to seeing those fledglings on our next visit, sometime in mid-July. I was ready for another racy walk in the woods with those two ladies.

Ivory-billed Woodpecker

One day my neighbor asked me whether I thought the reported sightings of the ivory-billed woodpecker were fact or fiction. I didn't give it much thought. My son and I were busy getting ready to attend Warbler Weekend in Frontenac over Mother's Day weekend. Because they were having difficulty finding speakers, I'd volunteered to give a talk on one of the two nights.

My talk, "In Defense of Crows," on Friday night was well received. I brought out a crow decoy from a cage, scattering a few crow feathers to add to the illusion. There was lots of laughter and some good questions. I was feeling pretty proud of myself until Saturday night rolled around.

That night the speaker was Jim Fitzpatrick, executive director of the Carpenter Nature Center, in Hastings, Minnesota. Like me, he's rather stocky and balding, only he has a shaggy gray moustache. He wore a white hooded sweatshirt. At least I'd worn a brand new tie for my crow talk. I thought Jim would give a review of activities at the Nature Center and how we'd all be welcome to come down and visit anytime. Wrong, warbler-breath!

Jim's younger brother, John, was the director of Cornell University's Lab of Ornithology. John and his colleagues had been involved in the search for the ivory-billed woodpecker since February 2004, and Jim had volunteered to help in the effort.

Jim showed slides of the Cache River National Wildlife Refuge in northeastern Arkansas where he had spent most of his vacation time since early 2004. He said he'd given his presentation many times before, but had been sworn to secrecy—until now—about the results of the search. Since the news had been leaked to the press a few days earlier, this was the first time he was able to publicly say that they'd found the bird! He was free to tell the whole story.

I'm sure the entire audience shared the same tingle of anticipation I felt. The excitement was warranted. Jim's slides showed cypress trees and stumps in a flooded forest. Navigation by canoe looked pretty dicey, and Jim's description of walking and wading through the swampy, humid muck, sometimes chest deep, was harrowing. The bayou is full of deadly cottonmouth water moccasins, alligators, huge spiders, and other nasty surprises.

Jim was essentially a pack mule for the scientists. One of his jobs was to replace the batteries on the remote acoustic monitoring equipment strapped to trees for recording ivory-bill raps and calls. The equipment was battery powered and the batteries had to be replaced every so often. Each morning his group got GPS coordinates for certain acoustic monitors and then set out by canoe to find and replace the batteries and lug the old ones back. These weren't flashlight batteries or NiCads. No, these were forty-pound car batteries.

Sometimes Jim was the canoeist for a scientist who shot video as they paddled through the bayou. One morning, Jim suggested to the camera-toting scientist that he might have better luck staying in one spot for the day, and Jim would come back to pick him up in the afternoon. The guy agreed, so Jim dropped the scientist off on a spongy, matted hump in the swamp and set off on his own to do some exploring.

At lunchtime, Jim lodged his canoe against a fallen cypress snag and began to unwrap a sandwich. Just then a very large woodpecker flew over the trees into the opening above the pool where he sat and then flew along the edge of the bayou before disappearing over the trees on the other side. Jim was stunned. He told us he was very sure it wasn't a pileated woodpecker. He had seen white areas on both the upper and underside of the wing in patterns that were definitely not a pileated pattern.

After what seemed like long minutes of hesitation and indecision, Jim decided to follow the bird to see if he could get a close up view. He paddled down the bayou, but didn't see it again. He returned to his lunch spot, jotted down notes of his observation and sketched what he had seen, then took a GPS reading of the location. Jim's sighting was one of fifteen or more during the Cornell search of the Cache River area. What a thrill! And to think I'd wowed the crowd with my crow talk. Fame is indeed fleeting.

In *The Grail Bird: Hot on the Trail of the Ivory-Billed Woodpecker*, by Tim Gallagher, Gallagher interviewed everybody he could find who claimed to have seen or heard an ivory-billed woodpecker. In early 2004, he and a friend actually saw an ivory-bill and started the intense search that Cornell helped to sponsor. Gallagher covers the story of Fitzpatrick's sighting with more detail and with salty quotations. It's a very good and compelling read.

To answer my neighbor's question: I do believe the ivory-billed woodpecker has been rediscovered, brought back from a perceived extinction. As Jim Fitzpatrick concluded in his talk, the bird seems to do well in environments where people don't like to go.

Now it's up to people to figure out ways to protect that environment and prevent putting this magnificent creature on the extinct list for real.

Nests I Have Known

Spring and early summer are the time of year to look for birds' nests, if you can find them. They're usually hidden from view by all the leaves covering the trees. But you can discover a nesting site by tracking birds carrying nesting materials—string, bits of cloth, sticks, grasses, even litter tossed on the ground by careless humans. Or you can watch for birds carrying food to their hungry, noisy youngsters.

I did just that one morning in late May when I led a St. Paul Audubon field trip to an area called the Ramsey County Open Space. I first looked for a completed nest I'd seen on a trip ten days earlier. A robin had landed in a muddy area, and I thought perhaps it was building a nest. Robins finish the insides of their nests with a thin layer of mud. So I watched as it flew to a nearby dead tree. It didn't have leaves or bark, so the nest was very visible in the main crook of the tree. I saw four hungry baby bird mouths sticking out of the nest. The robin hadn't been gathering mud, but rather, some tasty tidbits for its babies.

When I found the nest on the second visit, it was cocked to the side, empty, and quite disheveled. Possibly, it was too exposed and was raided by a predator, but a more hopeful explanation was that the young had fledged. They're usually ready to fly in fourteen to sixteen days after hatching. They could have flown by then.

Then we began to find other nests. The first, and one of the most dramatic belonged to a ruby-throated hummingbird. One field trip member spotted a hummingbird and watched it fly right to the nest, where it perched on the top of a branch some thirty feet up in a box elder tree. The nest looked like it had been plastered to the branch. Ruby-throated hummingbirds start with little fragments of plant material and fashion them into a small cup less than two inches in diameter. The nest is thickly lined with down, held together with spider webs and camouflaged with flakes of lichen. It expands elastically as the eggs hatch and the hatchlings grow. Amazing, eh?

Farther down the trail, we saw a bird fly to the far side of a tree trunk and seemingly disappear. We waited for it to work its way around the tree, but it never did. We walked a bit beyond the tree to see more of the other side. Pretty soon a white-breasted nuthatch peeked out of a hole in the trunk. It had ducked into a nest cavity. We watched as both adults took turns bringing food to the youngsters hidden in the nest hole.

The bottom of the white-breasted nuthatch nest cavity is covered with flakes and strips of bark, even lumps of dirt, topped by a cup of finely shredded bark, grasses, and tiny roots. The cup is lined with soft fur, wool, hair, and feathers. An industrious building project indeed, all done by the female. If you have sheep, watch for lady white-breasted nuthatches plucking wool from their coats!

As we continued our hike, we spotted a starling perched way at the top of a dead snag and watched it pop into a hole near the top. Here was a starling that didn't depend on a human structure like a stoplight post or power pole for a nest site. Again, a pair was bringing food to the nest. The starlings' nest cavity is a messy collection of stems, leaves, and other plant material. The cup's lined with feathers, wool, and moss. Another wool snatcher. Watch those sheep.

Finally, we saw one of the truly classic bird nests of summer, that of the Baltimore oriole. It hung from the end of a cottonwood branch, high in the tree, with the male perched atop it. He attracted our eyes and, perched right above the nest, left no doubt whose nest it was.

The female oriole does most of the nest building, weaving a deep pendant pouch from long fibers she's pulled from plants and vines.

She uses hair, string, yarn, and any other fibrous material humans have left lying around. The rim of the nest is attached to forked twigs. Sometimes twigs extending down the sides have been woven into the structure. The six-inch-deep cup is lined with hair, down from plants, wool (again!), and fine grasses. She usually completes the nest in about four to eight days.

All five of these nests were made and then furnished by a bird using just its beak and feet, shaping it with its body. All that knowledge is instinctual, hard-wired. They've never seen it done before they build their first.

Now, that's amazing!

Baby Bird ID

A baby duckling or chick springs from the egg with a set of starter feathers, all downy and fluffy, running around on its little legs. That's called a precocial nestling.

When a typical baby songbird first squirms out of its shell, it's naked, blind and helpless. That's an altricial nestling, and they all look pretty much alike. There isn't a lot to go on to help in identifying the little one.

And that's a problem for many of the volunteers at the Wildlife Rehabilitation Center, according to my friend Phil. Many of the volunteers are student interns, with a large turnover among them. Fortunately, it isn't necessary to identify the species to decide what to feed it. They all get the same kind of "gruel," a slurry of kitten food, vitamins, cod liver oil, eggs, crickets, and yogurt run through a blender, and fed through a syringe, with feedings every fifteen to thirty minutes from dawn to dusk.

But while they all get the same kind of food at first, identification is important because it's helpful to keep similar species together in the incubator. Some birds do better in a group, with "friends and family." And there's something to be said for keeping the quieter ones apart from the classic "squawkers."

In order to help train their volunteers, Phil had his staff create an infant-juvenile bird identification guide. It's a photo guide that features at least five photos of each of the bird species the WRC typically receives in a year. Each series starts with a photo of the bird as young as possible, one with the bird's gaping maw, and at least three pictures showing the bird as it changes into its juvenile form.

When identifying a baby bird, there are several things that can offer clues to the species. Volunteers study the gape flanges, the edges of that big wide mouth, noting its color and any streaking. What's the shape of the bill? What color is the inside of the mouth? Does the nestling have pin feathers or fuzzy down? Is there any color apparent yet? Look at the toe placement: woodpeckers have two to the front, two to the back; songbirds have three to the front, one to the back.

As the nestling grows, the photo series shows how the bill shape changes from a broad-based triangular shape to the more slender bill of the adult. There may be changes in the color of the bill, the eyes, and legs. And, as the feathers develop, they will begin to take on the color of a juvenile bird. The photos also help the volunteers to estimate the age of the nestling and decide when it can move to more solid foods.

I've used the term "nestling" so far. There's an important distinction that Jenni makes when he talks about whether or not to bring in a found bird. A nestling is essentially confined to the nest, fed by its parents, unable to fly. It should stay in the nest. If you find a nestling on the ground, put it back in the nest if you can. It's not true that parents will reject a baby bird that's been touched by a human.

The mom and pop usually won't spend very much time feeding a nestling on the ground. There's too much risk for them to be there for very long. It's better if you can get it back into the nest. If you can't find the nest, you can use a small plastic dish (like for whipped topping) lined with toilet paper or tissue. Put the nestling in it and put the prefab nest back up into the tree. The parents should find the baby bird by its squawking and resume feeding it.

The advice changes once the nestling has gained weight and grown its first set of feathers. It's ready to fledge, leaving the nest as a fledgling. If you find a fledgling on the ground, be aware that it will be hopping around. It's not necessarily injured. It just can't fly well yet, but it needs to be able to get away from you and predators like your pets. The parents may still come down to feed it, but it's learning to find food on its own.

You should leave a fledgling alone, but with one exception: If you see it in the mouth of a cat, try to recover the bird and take it to a rehabilitation facility or call a veterinary clinic. Even if you don't see any obvious injuries, cats have septic mouths, and it's best to get the bird checked out. Keep cats inside during the fledging period. (Actually, it's best to keep them inside always.)

All the moms and dads in the bird world—and their injured offspring—will really appreciate it if you can tell the difference between a nestling and a fledgling.

Bittern Rescue

The phone rang on a Friday afternoon. "Is this the Birdman?" a woman asked.

When I replied I was indeed the Birdman of Lauderdale, she told me her husband was standing guard over a bittern down at the St. Anthony Park Community Gardens, not far from Lauderdale. It seemed to be sick or injured, she reasoned, because it didn't try to flee. She and her husband were about to leave town for the weekend and wanted to find someone who could get the bird to the Wildlife Rehabilitation Center.

This was an offer I couldn't refuse. Within minutes, I had grabbed our dog carrier and several towels. I tossed them in the car and quickly headed out.

The American bittern is a beautiful, but very shy denizen of marshes and wetlands. It's about two feet tall, with a dark back and a light brown streaked neck and front. It "freezes" when frightened, extending its neck and head straight up so it blends in with the surrounding cattails and rushes. If the reeds are moving in the wind, the bittern will even sway in rhythm to further conceal itself.

When I reached the gardens, I unloaded my gear and walked up to a fellow standing at the garden gate. He identified himself as Sherman Eagles. He'd been working in his family's garden plot when he noticed some movement in an adjoining plot. He thought it was the same bird he and his wife had seen earlier in the week in the prairie grasses next to the plots. The bird had been lying down under some raspberry canes until Sherman approached. Then it sat up. Sherman had backtracked, called his wife, and waited for me.

We gingerly retraced Sherman's steps to his plot, looked throughout both it and the adjoining plot, but there was no sign of the bittern. It seemed to have escaped. We searched the whole garden area and all the plots without success. I told Sherman I'd try to come back on the weekend.

Quite a few abandoned green tomatoes and some squash littered the area. I theorized the bird could find something to eat if it stayed in the gardens. The November weather was moderating somewhat with lows in the 30s and highs up to the 50s. I thought it should be all right for a day or two.

The next afternoon, Jean assisted me in the search for the injured bird. We started at the prairie restoration area and headed east, walking through the prairie. We continued along the railroad tracks, scanning the tall weeds until we came to the garden area where we climbed over the back fence. I went to retrieve the car while Jean started looking through the garden plots.

As I parked the car near the gardens, Jean stood in a corner plot waving her arms above her head. She had found the bittern. I got the dog carrier, the towels, and my protective goggles from the back of the car. I put on my leather gloves and stepped quietly along the plots until I got near to where Jean stood with a big smile on her face. There, scrunched down against the plot's low fence, was a soccer-ball-sized clump of brown feathers.

"Has it moved? Is it alive?" I mouthed toward her.

"Yes," she mouthed back. I crept toward the bird. It turned its head to face me, but made no other move. The view I had of that face made a strong impression: It had a bayonet of a bill with small eyes protruding on either side. It meant business!

I didn't see any obvious injury. When I got to within three or four feet, I lunged forward and smothered the bird's body with the towel. It made a loud, low-pitched, open-beaked growling hiss as I wrapped it up and headed toward the dog carrier.

Jean opened the carrier door, and as I began to put the bird into it, its head popped out from under the towel, making a stabbing pass at my face. Egrets, herons, and bitterns are infamous for going for the eyes of people who handle them. I was very glad I had goggles.

When we arrived at the Wildlife Center in nearby Roseville, a volunteer took the carrier to the back room and transferred the bittern to another cage. When she returned, she remarked that it seemed very light in weight. That suggested that it hadn't been eating well for a while. It was probably dehydrated, too. She said that the bittern also took a swipe at her face. "That's a good sign!" she said.

The center runs on donations. We've been there several times and always leave a contribution to help defer their costs. As I was writing out my check, I wryly asked how much a week the bittern's room and board would cost. She laughed and looked up the bittern diet.

This was an expensive menu. They're fed fish, mice, and insects. I abandoned my frivolous offer to cover a week of care and left a more modest amount. I'd been totally wrong about a bittern being able to subsist on tomatoes and squash in the garden plots. They're predominately carnivores, taking any fish, frogs, salamanders, small mammals, or insects they can grab. They slowly stalk their prey or stand in a frozen pose until something comes within range and then nail it with that dagger-like beak.

I received a call from Phil on Tuesday afternoon. Unfortunately, he said, the bittern had to be put down; its injuries were too severe. He'd have the vet call me to answer any questions I had.

Dr. Karen Shenoy called me the next day. The bird had had a compound fracture of its right wing bone. The exposed ends of the bone had been contaminated with soil and were necrotic. You can picture the injury by imagining the way a hollow chicken bone breaks, with lots of splintery, jagged ends. Dr. Shenoy told me that there was no way to repair the fracture that would leave the bird pain-free, let alone able to fly again. Euthanasia was the kindest option.

She also said there was no indication of impact with an automobile, no head injury. We hypothesized that the bittern may have hit a wire during its nocturnal migration flight. Little is know about bitterns, but biologists believe they migrate singly at night. By the time someone finds an injured creature and gets it in for treatment, it's usually in bad shape. It's been spending its time avoiding predators, trying to stay hidden, and probably not eating very well.

My friend Val volunteered at the Wildlife Center for a number of years. She told me their philosophy is that a sick or injured critter that comes to the center is released one way or the other, back to the wild or, if it can't be rehabilitated, released from its pain.

That's some solace.

The Grebe that Wouldn't Leave

It was December. The days were getting colder, and the open water on Bennett Lake in Roseville was shrinking. A small bird swam and dove out among the mallards.

On their daily walks around the lake with their dogs, Dr. Kent Kokko and Maggie Moris had seen the grebe all summer and wondered why it hadn't migrated for the sunny South.

Maggie said, "In November, when the migrations were almost done, and it was still around, I thought this isn't good. In December, when the lake started to freeze over, I thought this is going to be a problem."

They identified the bird as a pied-billed grebe. Many folks they met on the lake path asked if they'd seen the baby loon. Maggie would tell them it was a pied-billed grebe, and folks would allow they'd never seen one before.

The pied-billed grebe's usual fall migration period runs from mid-August through mid-December with a peak in mid-October. A few winter over in Minnesota each year, but they need open water for food and mobility. Their diet consists of aquatic insects and invertebrates, small fish, and crustaceans. They're extremely clumsy on land with legs placed far back under the body like a loon's.

Why was this grebe still hanging around? Kent surmised, "Since it had hung out with the mallards, it began to identify with mallards, and decided to stay as long as there was open water, and then it became trapped. Mallards can just fly off the ice." The grebe needed open water to get a running start before take off. "Well, the grebe made a tragic mistake," he said.

Kent and Maggie waited and watched each day as the lake began to freeze until only certain areas of open water remained where the grebe could swim and dive for food. Each night it was getting colder and colder, and the area of open water was getting smaller and smaller. The grebe sought sanctuary in a small pool underneath some branches hanging down into the water. One night the ice began to form along the shore. Still the grebe didn't leave. The weather forecast was grim. "A cold snap is coming," Maggie said, "and the lake is going to freeze over."

Early on the evening of December 15th, they made their first rescue attempt. Kent taped a short-handled fishing net to an extension pole. The pool of open water had shrunk to less than four feet in diameter. One mallard swam with the grebe. Since the ice was too thin to support a person, Kent worked the net from shore. The mallard took off immediately as Kent attempted to coax the net under the grebe.

The bird became very agitated, dove under the water repeatedly, but with nowhere to go, would bob up again. Then it panicked and jumped out onto the ice, scooting its way toward a group of mallards farther out on the ice. Kent and Maggie decided to abandon the rescue attempt.

Maggie was afraid the grebe would have a hard time getting back to the water hole since he was so awkward on the ice. She didn't sleep well the next few nights. The cold weather continued. She'd wake up at two in the morning, see how cold it was and think, "Oh, that poor little grebe is still out there."

On the morning of December 18th, they saw that temperatures were expected to drop all day to a low near zero with strong northerly winds. They felt they had to try one more time, or the bird wasn't going to make it. Before sunrise, they headed over to the lake, bringing the same long-handled net. This time, however, Maggie went out onto the ice on the far side of the pool to close the bird's prior avenue of escape. Kent again worked the net from shore.

There was just enough light to see what they were doing. Kent could get the net under the grebe, but it would dive over or under it. He had very little room to maneuver around the branches hanging down into the little pool. Finally, he decided to wait him out. He held the net below the surface of the water until the grebe popped up over the net. When it finally did, Kent lifted the net up into the air, and the grebe dropped to the bottom.

There were more branches than bird in the net. Kent handed the pole and net over to Maggie and let her untangle it and carry it back to shore, ice cracking beneath her as she walked. They'd thought to bring along a box with a towel in the bottom. Maggie lowered the net, grebe and all, into the box. Then she held the bird while Kent worked the net off its feet and head. "He wasn't grateful!" Maggie said. "He was a very ungrateful bird!"

He kept pecking at her finger. He couldn't break the skin, so she let him focus on the finger. Once home, they put the box in the bathroom with the lights out and waited for the doors of the Wildlife Rehabilitation Center to open at 9 a.m. They dropped off the grebe, headed home, and took their dogs for another walk around the lake.

Maggie posted a sign to let others know what had happened to the grebe. In the hour and a half after the rescue, the ice had begun to close the little pool. Within two hours, the lake had frozen over completely. The pool was no more.

Later on they heard from the veterinarian, Dr. Karen King, that the bird appeared to be in good health with good muscle tone. It was still feisty. There was a very good reason he hadn't migrated. He only had one wing! The right one was missing. The humerus (the upper arm in a human) was cut off about a half inch below the shoulder joint.

It wasn't a recent injury. Maybe earlier in the summer a snapping turtle had tried to make a meal of the little guy and only got an appetizer. There were some scapular feathers extending along that side of its body. It wasn't obvious that the wing was missing until it was examined closely.

Thanks go to Kent and Maggie for their persistent attempts to rescue this stranded pied-billed grebe and for giving him a chance to live. During his rehabilitation at the WRC, he ate well, dove in his own small, private pool, and preferred to be left alone. Several months of rehabilitation later, a permanent home was found for him at Chicago's Lincoln Park Zoo, where he wouldn't have to worry about being frozen into the ice.